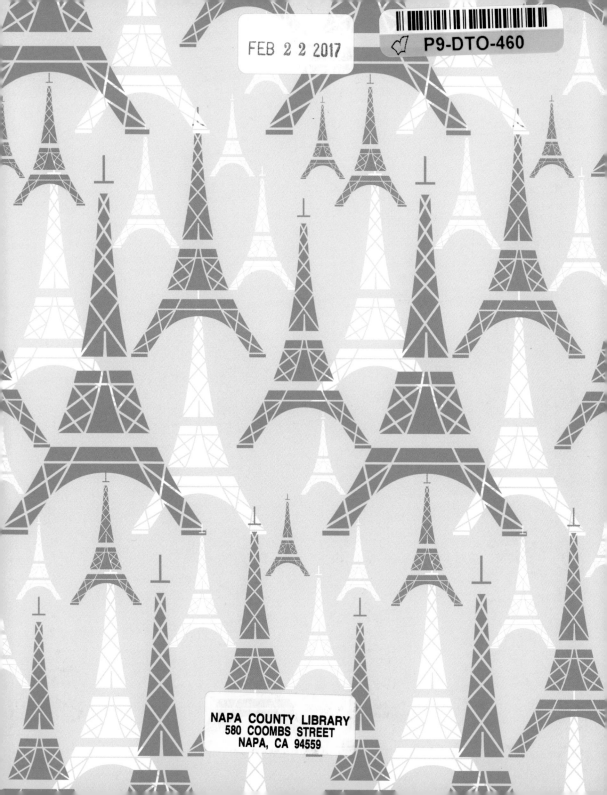

PARIS PRECINCTS

A curated guide to the city's best shops, eateries, bars and other hangouts

PARIS
PRECINCTS

A curated guide to the city's
best shops, eateries, bars and
other hangouts

DONNA WHEELER

hardie grant publishing

CONTENTS

Bienvenue to *Paris Precincts*! Welcome also to Paris, the world's most fabled city, which draws more visitors than any other. This book is designed to inspire you to wander the city's boulevards and backstreets, to discover new neighbourhoods and explore with a fresh eye those that may already be familiar.

Just a decade or so ago, Paris was seen as stuck in its ways, tired, touristy and conservative. Not so today – the city is exploding with a youthful, exuberant and irreverent energy. In some neighbourhoods it seems like a new café, restaurant or cocktail bar opens every week; likewise shops selling the wares of young designers and artisans are popping up in streets once the preserve of butchers and bakers. I've selected a snapshot of places that are part of this blossoming scene, along with a number of evergreens, eccentrics and surprises.

My Paris is always a mix of these sometimes opposing, sometimes complementary forces: I adore the thrill of the new, the cool, the now, but also long for the comfort and deep satisfaction of the traditional, the rough-around-the-edges and the true local's haunts. No book can be totally comprehensive, so I encourage you to use my suggestions to strike out, roam wide and dig deep, be it by arrondissement or street, or via chef, barista or designer, and claim Paris as your own.

Donna Wheeler

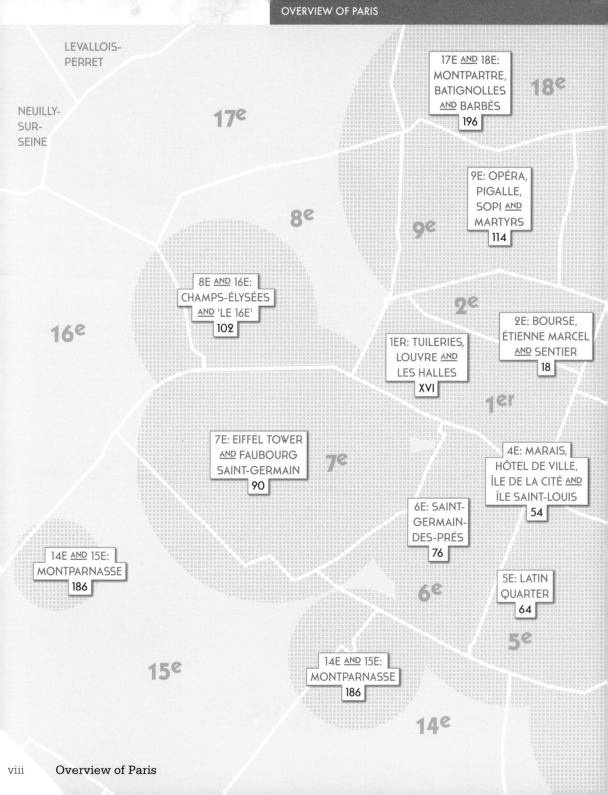

LEVALLOIS-
PERRET

NEUILLY-
SUR-
SEINE

17ᵉ

18ᵉ

17E AND 18E:
MONTPARTRE,
BATIGNOLLES
AND BARBÈS
196

8ᵉ

9ᵉ

**9E: OPÉRA,
PIGALLE,
SOPI AND
MARTYRS**
114

16ᵉ

**8E AND 16E:
CHAMPS-ÉLYSÉES
AND 'LE 16E'**
102

2ᵉ

**2E: BOURSE,
ÉTIENNE MARCEL
AND SENTIER**
18

**1ER: TUILERIES,
LOUVRE AND
LES HALLES**
XVI

1ᵉʳ

7ᵉ

**7E: EIFFEL TOWER
AND FAUBOURG
SAINT-GERMAIN**
90

**4E: MARAIS,
HÔTEL DE VILLE,
ÎLE DE LA CITÉ AND
ÎLE SAINT-LOUIS**
54

**6E: SAINT-
GERMAIN-
DES-PRÉS**
76

**14E AND 15E:
MONTPARNASSE**
186

6ᵉ

**5E: LATIN
QUARTER**
64

5ᵉ

15ᵉ

**14E AND 15E:
MONTPARNASSE**
186

14ᵉ

PANTIN

LE PRÉ-
SAINT-
GERVAIS

ROMAINVILLE

LES LILAS

19ᵉ

19E AND 20E:
BELLEVILLE AND
MÉNILMONTANT
210

10ᵉ

10E: CANAL SAINT MARTIN,
RÉPUBLIQUE AND
FAUBOURG SAINT-DENIS
130

BAGNOLET

20ᵉ

3ᵉ

3E: MARAIS AND
HAUT-MARAIS
32

11ᵉ

11E: BASTILLE,
CHARONNE AND
OBERKAMPF
148

19E AND 20E:
BELLEVILLE AND
MÉNILMONTANT
210

4ᵉ

MONTREUIL

12E: ALIGRE,
BERCY AND THE
COULÉE VERTE
164

VINCENNES

12ᵉ

13E: PLACE D'ITALIE,
GOBELINS AND
QUAI D'AUSTERLITZ
176

13ᵉ

SAINT-
MANDÉ

PARIS

For many centuries the city of Paris was but a densely wound, walled settlement on the Seine's Île de la Cité, with marshlands to the north and fields and vineyards to the south. Its vaguely snail-shell-shaped blob is still remarkably compact – home to a little over 2 million of greater Paris' 12 million or so inhabitants – although the map you navigate by today tells a story of rapid development from the medieval period onwards.

That snail shape, a volute if you will, has been divided into administrative areas called arrondissements since the French Revolution. From 1860, when Baron Haussmann razed and rebuilt much of old Paris, and pushed the city boundaries out to its former fortifications, there have been 20 numbered arrondissements spiraling out in a clockwise direction from the centre's 'premier' arrondissement or 1er.

That said, older Parisians can still recall a time when everyone thought of themselves as belonging to a 'quartier', or quarter, which either referred back to the pre-Revolution parish districts or sometimes the four smaller districts into which each arrondissement is divided. For hundreds of years these quartiers were where one was born, worked, shopped, socialised and often died. But in the years after WW II, as daily life moved beyond these tight village-like communities, each arrondissement took on its own broad identity as well.

Paris Precincts' chapters are divided into these arrondissements, mostly a single one but sometimes two, and I've used the French 'e' suffix after each arrondissement number, which is the abbreviation of '-eme' (as in deuxième, troisième; i.e. second, third etc.). In the case of the 1st arrondissement, the abbreviation 'er' is used, short for 'premier'. Arrondissement numbers also appear as the last two digits in Parisian postcodes.

Each chapter is also headed up with a few neighbourhood names, a somewhat random collection of traditional quartiers, landmarks or major streets. These are not exhaustive – there are many subdistricts in each arrondissement, not to mention landmarks – but they are the most useful for travellers.

The city's other great geographical and social divider is the Seine, giving the city its 'rive gauche' and 'rive droite' – the Left Bank and Right Bank. While these were once indicative of social status and mores – the Left tending to bohemian, intellectual and, in parts, poor, while the Right was the centre of power and commerce – these distinctions, always rather blurred, have, over time, come to mean very little. Current chroniclers of the city point out that a more obvious, if still rather reductive, division today runs east to west, with the eastern half being the playground of the young and fashionable, and home to significant immigrant communities, while the west is overwhelmingly where the wealthy and traditionally powerful reside.

Life in Paris contains many beautiful, fascinating contradictions. It's an undeniably modern, progressive world capital, one that in the last ten years has seen rapid gentrification along with an influx of globally aware, and not necessarily French, restaurateurs, shop owners, hoteliers and entrepreneurs. It's a city that feels like pure fantasy, a waking dream, for many visitors, but is, at the same time, a defiantly real, deeply complex and occasionally troubled place. It retains a profound, multilayered sense of self, and continues doggedly and delightfully in its traditional daily rhythms among the ghosts of history that live on, wherever you may turn.

THE FAMOUS FIVE

Eiffel Tower, 7e
Gustave Eiffel's 1889 iron-latticed tower needs no introduction.

Notre-Dame de Paris, 4e
A French Gothic wonder of flying buttresses, gargoyles and sacred geometry, this 850-year-old cathedral is Paris' enduring heart.

The Louvre, 1er
One of the world's largest art museums, the Musée du Louvre is glorious, exhausting and absolutely unmissable.

Sacré-Cœur, 18e
Built in a spirit of conservative piety (and questionable taste), this towering, white, late-19th-century basilica boasts Paris' best views.

Cimetière du Père-Lachaise, 20e
The leafy boulevards of this cemetery are lined with the graves and mausoleums of some of last century's greatest thinkers, artists and musicians.

PARKS AND GARDENS

Jardin des Tuileries, 1er
Jardin du Luxembourg, 6e
Parc de Belleville, 20e
Parc des Buttes Chaumont, 19e
Bois de Boulogne, 16e
Parc de la Villette, 19e
Bois de Vincennes, 12e

MODERN ART

Centre Pompidou, 4e
Houses the Musée National d'Art Moderne in a splendid, if controversial, 20th-century building.

Musée de l'Orangerie, 1er
Home to eight of Monet's luminous *Water Lilies* paintings, sublimely shimmering between abstraction and representation.

Musée d'Orsay, 7e
The works of the Impressionists, post-Impressionists and much underrated Nabis occupy this former train station by the Seine.

Musée d'Art Moderne, 16e
European and international art of the 20th century, as well as monographic contemporary shows – usually no queues.

FASHION, DESIGN AND INTERIORS

Musée des Arts Décoratifs, 1er
In a grand annexe of the Louvre, a fabulous collection of design and fashion.

Galerie-Musée Baccarat, 16e
A surreal Philippe Starck refit of a legendary maison particuliere (private house) filled with Baccarat crystal.

Fondation Pierre Bergé – Yves Saint Laurent, 16e
YSL's haute couture legacy lives on in this wonderful museum.

Palais Galliera, 16e
Great themed fashion exhibitions in a dramatic setting.

CULTURE AND HISTORY

Musée du quai Branly, 7e
France's post-colonial assembly of indigenous art of Africa, Asia, Oceania and the Americas housed in a vertical, garden-clad building by Jean Nouvel.

Institut du Monde Arabe (IMA), 5e
Beautiful collections of North African and Middle Eastern objects and artworks in another Jean Nouvel masterpiece.

Musée Carnavalet, 3e
The city of Paris' own exquisite social history museum, with particularly wonderful documents and objects from the French Revolution.

Musée National du Moyen Âge, 5e
The highlight of this museum of medieval history is the delightfully allegorical *Lady with the Unicorn* tapestry series.

Musée de la Chasse et de la Nature, 3e
Two 17th-century mansions house a collection of paintings, taxidermy and a host of fabulous curiosities in this surprisingly seductive museum of hunting and nature. A stylist's dream.

CONTEMPORARY ART

Palais de Tokyo, 16e
The city's largest and often most-challenging contemporary art space, housed in a 1930s monument.

Fondation Louis Vuitton, 16e
Frank Gehry's brash, free-form, 21st-century building houses the LV director's stunning contemporary art collection in the Bois de Boulogne.

Jeu de Paume, 8e
France's national photographic and media art institution, known for its cutting-edge, intellectual shows.

Fondation Cartier, 14e
Contemporary art in another beautiful Jean Nouvel–designed building.

Maison Rouge, 12e
Monographic shows from younger contemporary artists in an old industrial print works.

Monnaie de Paris, 6e
Site-specific installations by leading international artists in the city's old mint.

FESTIVALS

We Love Green, 16e
Indie festival in the Jardins de Bagatelle in May.

Nuit des Musées
Paris' museums open until midnight and offer free entry in this country-wide event in May.

Fête de la Musique
Street music festival held on 21 June right across Paris and France.

Rock en Seine, 16e
Huge summer rock and indie festival in Saint-Cloud in late August.

Nuit Blanche
Free contemporary art festival in October, with selected museums and events open all night.

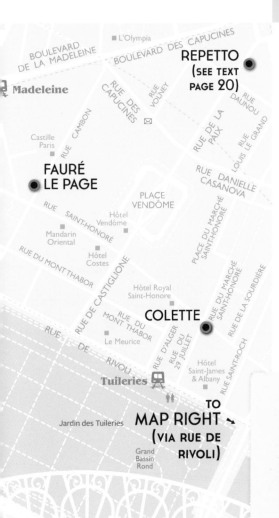

'Le Premier' arrondissement is Paris' grand beating heart. Much of this Seine-facing strip is given over to the stately Tuileries – the one-time garden of former queen Catherine de' Medici and a public park since the French Revolution – and the equally historic and equally expansive Louvre museum.

Across the rue de Rivoli from these landmarks are the shopping golden mile of rue Saint-Honoré and the Palais Royal, a regal 17th-century former palace complex with one of Paris' prettiest gardens and, within its colonnades, some of the city's most fashionable shops, cafes and restaurants. Les Halles was the city's legendary produce market until the 1970s. Reborn as the drab shopping mall Forum des Halles, it's currently undergoing a major renovation.

24   JUN 8876

SHOP

1 ASTIER DE VILLATTE
2 FAURÉ LE PAGE
3 YASMINE ESLAMI
4 MAISON KITSUNÉ
5 LES SALONS DU PALAIS ROYAL SERGE LUTENS
6 COLETTE

7 ÉPICE
8 E. DEHILLERIN (see map p. 019)

EAT

9 TÉLESCOPE
10 CLAUS
11 CAFÉ KITSUNÉ
12 KUNITORAYA UDON

1ER: TUILERIES, LOUVRE AND LES HALLES

Square de
Louvois

2e

RUE GALLON
RUE MARSOLLIER
RUE DALAYRAC
RUE MÉHUL
RUE SAINTE-ANNE
RUE CHÉRUBINI
RUE RAMEAU
RUE DE RICHELIEU
RUE VIVIENNE
RUE DE LA BANQUE

PASSAGE
CHOISEUL

RUE DES PETITS CHAMPS

RUE DE VENTADOUR
RUE DES MOULINS
RUE CHABANAIS

Hôtel
Opéra
Maintenon

AVENUE DE L'OPÉRA

RUE THÉRÈSE

Hôtel Louvre
Saint-Anne

RUE VILLEDO

RUE DE BEAUJOLAIS

GALERIE
VIVIENNE

RUE DE LA FEUILLADE

RUE DES PETITS CHAMPS

**MAISON
KITSUNÉ**

**VERJUS &
VERJUS
BAR À VINS**

🚇
Pyramides

TÉLESCOPE

Hôtel
Thérèse

**KUNITORAYA
UDON**

ELLSWORTH

STELLA
MCCARTNEY

RUE RADZIWILL

RUE LA VRILLIÈRE

AVENUE DE L'OPÉRA

RUE DES PYRAMIDES

RUE D'ARGENTEUIL

RUE SAINTE-ANNE

**YASMINE
ESLAMI**

STÉPHANE
CHAPELLE

**CAFÉ
KITSUNÉ**

N

RUE DE VALOIS

TO
E. DEHILLERIN
(SEE MAP
PAGE 19)

1er

RUE MOLIÈRE

RUE DE RICHELIEU

RUE DE MONTPENSIER

LE POMPON

Hôtel
Montpensier

Jardin du
Palais Royal

**ASTIER DE
VILLATTE**

RUE DE L'ÉCHELLE

Hôtel
Normandy

PLACE
ANDRÉ
MALRAUX

Comédie
Française

ÉPICE

**Palais
Royal**

Cour
d'Honneur

**LES SALONS
DU PALAIS ROYAL
SERGE LUTENS**

PLACE DE VALOIS

RUE DES BONS ENFANTS

RUE DU COLONEL DRIANT

RUE
MONTESQUIEU

RUE SAINT-HONORÉ

Cour
de l'Horloge

EAT AND DRINK

13 ELLSWORTH
14 VERJUS & VERJUS BAR À
VINS

JUN 2016

RUE DE RIVOLI

Hôtel
du Louvre

TO
**FAURÉ
LE PAGE,
COLLETTE
& REPETTO**
(SEE MAP LEFT)

PLACE DU PALAIS ROYAL

🚇
**Palais
Royal–
Musee du
Louvre**

RUE DE VALOIS

RUE DE RIVOLI

RUE SAINT-HONORÉ

CLAUS

RUE DU PÉLICAN

RUE JEAN-JACQUES ROUSSEAU

RUE DE MARENGO

Temple
de l'Oratoire
du Louvre

RUE DE L'ORATOIRE

Place du
Carrousel

PLACE DU CARROUSEL

Louis
XIV
statue

Pyramide

**Musée
du Louvre**

Jardin
de l'Oratoire

RUE DE RIVOLI

🚇
**Louvre–
Rivoli**

Cour
Napoleon

Cour
Carrée

Cour
Lefuel

Cour
Visconti

0   50 m

001

1.

ASTIER DE VILLATTE

173 rue Saint-Honoré
01 42 60 74 13
astierdevillatte.com
Open Mon–Sat 11am–7pm
Metro: Tuileries, Palais Royal–
Musée du Louvre

The milky-glazed black ceramic tableware and scented candles of Astier de Villatte can be found throughout the world, but if you're enchanted by Ivan Pericoli and Benoît Astier de Villatte's wistful aesthetic, a dedicated visit to the brand's Parisian home is a must. Once a silversmith's shop frequented by Napoleon, little has changed in the tiny space since then – its creaking wooden shelves and faded wallpaper make the ethereal plates, cups and sculptural pieces seem all the more precious and mysterious. Surreal and whimsical window displays often highlight a recent collaboration, while in the back room sigh-inducing dinner sets sit stacked.

FAURÉ LE PAGE

21 rue Cambon
01 49 27 99 36
faurelepage.com
Open Mon–Fri 10am–7pm
Metro: Tuileries, Pyramides

- -

Once Louis XVI's armourer of choice, Fauré le Page was also celebrated by writers such as Balzac and Dumas for handing out sabres, swords and muskets to the Parisian working-class revolutionaries during the French Revolution. While its finely crafted weapons may have fallen out of fashion sometime last century, in 2013 Augustin de Buffévent reimagined the venerable house as a small leather goods company, its bags and accessories drawing inspiration from Fauré le Page's original storage and carriage kits. Totes, handbags, wallets and luggage have a dominant palette of grey, mustard, deep green, brown and navy blue. They're a picture of restraint, but, like the velvet-draped, taxidermy-embellished shop, have the odd deliciously high-camp flourish thrown in.

3.

YASMINE ESLAMI
35 rue de Richelieu
09 84 51 51 14
yasmine-eslami.com
Open Tues–Sat 2–7pm, or
by appointment
Metro: Palais Royal–Musée du
Louvre, Pyramides

Yasmine Eslami, a Vivienne
Westwood alumnus and one
of France's most sought after
stylists, quietly launched her
lingerie line a few years back.
Word of mouth and some
smart international online
retailers ensured her tulle,
lace, cotton voile and jersey
pieces graced the curves of
in-the-know women around
the world in no time. Just
like her sheer triangle bras
and low-cut knickers, this
beguiling little black-walled
shop eschews any hint of
frou-frou boudoir, instead
conjuring a deeply sexy, '70s
rock'n'roll vibe. Try it all on –
Eslami's knack for fit might
just give you some pleasant
cleavage surprises.

4.

MAISON KITSUNÉ
52 rue de Richelieu
01 42 60 34 28
kitsune.fr
Open Mon–Sat 11am–7.30pm
Metro: Pyramides, Bourse

Kitsuné – the Franco-
Japanese fashion-music
love child of Gildas Loaëc
(one-time manager of Daft
Punk) and architect Masaya
Kuroki – got famous on the
back of its Zeitgeisty music
compilations championing
the likes of Bloc Party, La
Roux, Phoenix and Hot Chip
back in the early noughties.
Fashion-wise, the label has
what insiders call 'hanger
appeal', hitting the sweet
spot between classic and
street, smart and fun,
Japanese preppy and French
effortlessness. Caps, sloppy
joes and accessories gleefully
sport Parisian slogans and
the occasional Eiffel Tower
(souvenir and gift alert!).
The growing empire now
takes in Tokyo, Hong Kong
and New York, and there's
a huge boulevard des Filles
du Calvaire shop (in the
3e; *see map* p. 033), but
this little original remains a
sentimental favourite.

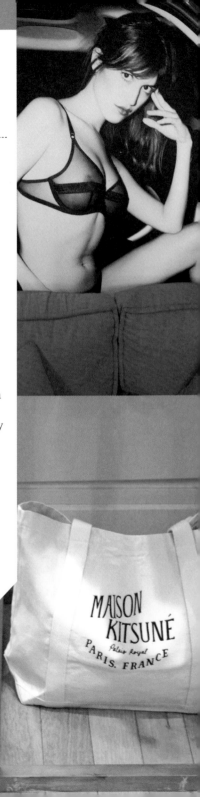

3.

3.

3.

4.

4.

4.

5.

LES SALONS DU PALAIS ROYAL SERGE LUTENS

142 Galerie de Valois,
Palais Royal
01 49 27 09 09
sergelutens.com
Open Mon–Sat 10am–7pm
Metro: Bourse, Pyramides

- -

Serge Lutens, one of France's
most original perfumers,
came to scent after careers
as a designer, stylist,
photographer, filmmaker
and consultant to the likes of
Christian Dior and Shiseido.
Established in 1992, this salon
was one of the first new shops
in the Palais Royal. Its decor,
a glowing violet and black
cocoon of friezes, panelling
and infinity mirrors, is a
wonderful way to encounter
Lutens' unconventional,
complex and story-filled
perfumes, like the classic,
unisex Gris Clair – a medicinal
lavender fragrance warmed
by amber and tonka bean
and deepened with smoky
incense. Keep an eye out for
the limited editions that are
released yearly, only available
at the salon – snap one up
and, for added luxury, have
your initials etched onto
the bottle.

COLETTE

213 rue Saint-Honoré
01 55 35 33 90
colette.fr
Open Mon–Sat 11am–7pm
Metro: Tuileries, Pyramides

Paris' original curated concept store, Colette is now in her (yes, she's definitely a she) second decade. More than anywhere else, this was the place that came to symbolise the city's rebirth of cool, its pumped-up soundtrack bringing a new, young audience to the once frump-luxe Saint-Honoré strip. Be it trainers, Alaïa ankle boots, iPhone cases or art- and design-focused books, everything in the store is there because of the gut instinct of creative director, Sarah Andelman, and her team – and it's as visionary a mix of goods as ever. The see-and-be-seen action centres on the ground floor, with its boy-magnet gadgets and ever-changing exhibitions, leaving the fashion-filled floor above a blissfully peaceful place to browse.

7.

ÉPICE

27–28 Galerie de Montpensier,
Palais Royal
01 42 96 68 26
epice.com
Open Tues–Sat 11am–7pm
Metro: Pyramides

- -

A Parisian accessories
house with Danish
natives Bess Nielsen and Jan
Machenhauer at the helm,
Épice sells linen, cotton,
silk, wool and cashmere
scarves that are the perfect
combination of Nordic
earthiness, French finery and
Indian craftsmanship. Each
piece has an enveloping
softness, and colours and
patterns subtly reference the
palettes of Danish painters
Vilhelm Hammershoi and
Michael Peter Ancher, the
seascapes of Skagen and the
streets of Copenhagen. The
shop also stocks a range of
elaborately woven Italian-
made cardigans, jumpers and
gloves. With its inky walls
and rows of wooden drawers,
it feels as if it's always been a
Palais Royal feature.

8.

E. DEHILLERIN

18–20 rue Coquillière
01 42 36 53 13
eshop.e-dehillerin.fr
Open Mon 9am–12.30pm &
2–6pm, Tues–Sat 9am–6pm
Metro: Louvre-Rivoli, Les Halles

- -

This packed-to-the-rafters
cookware shop, dating back
to the 1820s, is a legacy of
when chefs shopped for
their daily ingredients at
Les Halles, the city's main
produce market, then popped
in here for, say, a new pot
or rolling pin. Cooks of all
persuasions, from experts to
happy amateurs, will get that
little thrill that only seeing
so much cookware in one
spot can bring. Copper pans,
pots and pastry bowls can be
found in the basement and
the baking equipment near
the entrance. Don't expect
bargains, but you'll definitely
find unique things here, from
tiny fluted tartlet moulds
to a whopping galetiere
for turning out perfect
Breton galettes (savoury
buckwheat pancakes).

PARIS TIP

The Louvre's Musée des Arts Décoratifs houses what might be the world's best design and fashion collections. Art Nouveau and Art Deco devotees will be particularly pleased, but the museum's holdings stretch back as far as the 13th century.

9.

TÉLESCOPE

5 rue Villedo
01 42 61 33 14
telescopecafe.com
Open Mon–Fri 8.30am–5pm,
Sat 9.30am–6.30pm
Metro: Pyramides

One of the vanguard figures in Paris' coffee revolution, Nicolas Clerc still often mans his Marzocco espresso machine at Télescope, turning out perfect café noisettes (macchiatos) and café crèmes from locally roasted beans. Nic and his band of bilingual customers are always up for a chat. 'I baked the financiers myself. Do you think they're moist enough?' he may enquire when you come to pay your bill. Delightfully unassuming, Télescope is, however, a firm favourite with the city's coffee cognoscenti – if the tiny tables are all taken, grab your order to go and head to the sublimely pretty, rose-filled garden of the nearby Palais Royal.

10.

CLAUS

14 rue Jean-Jacques Rousseau
01 42 33 55 10
claus-paris.net
Open Mon–Fri 8am–5pm,
Sat–Sun 9.30am–5pm
Metro: Palais Royal–Musée du Louvre, Les Halles

Former fashion PR consultant Claus Estermann has brought Bavaria's breakfast to Paris – a formidable spread of boiled eggs, ham, Saint-Nectaire cheese, bread, stone-fruit compote and cake – although his chic forest-green-and-white café has plenty of other options if you're of a daintier persuasion. The muesli is spot on and there's an array of pastries, biscuits and tarts. Coffee here is good too, making it a morning meeting favourite of the local fashion-industry set. Estermann's épicerie du petit-déjeuner (breakfast grocery), across the road, sells his baked goods to take away, or ask the staff there to make you up a picnic for your hotel room or the park.

9.

9.

9.

9.

10.

10.

11.

CAFÉ KITSUNÉ

51 Galerie de Montpensier,
Palais Royal
01 40 15 62 31
kitsune.fr
Open Mon–Sun 8.30am–6.30pm
Metro: Pyramides, Bourse

This intimate stand-up coffee bar, with brews care of London's Workshop Coffee Co., makes for a charming Palais Royal rest stop. The baristas are mostly Australian or Australian-trained (yes, they do know their espressos and piccolos), and there's a welcoming, no-worries vibe that you don't expect among all the Palais Royal splendour. Noglu – a local gluten-free baker – ships in addictive green-tea-chocolate-chip cookies, moist carrot cake and crisp little shortbread foxes (kitsuné means fox in Japanese), while Paris' juice king Bob's supplies cold-pressed juices. As if a loll by the Palais Royal fountain could get any more delightful, there are also ice-cream and sorbets to go in summer.

PARIS TIP
The Palais Royal's Les Deux Plateaux art installation by Daniel Buren comprises 260 black-and-white candy-striped marble columns. A controversial commission back in 1986, today it is a favourite with kissing couples, skateboarders and selfie-takers.

KUNITORAYA UDON
1 rue Villedo
01 47 03 33 65
kunitoraya.com
Open Thurs–Tues 11am–3pm &
6–11pm
Metro: Pyramides

Japanese cooking has long had a foothold in Paris, with the restaurants and grocers of rue Saint-Anne known as Little Tokyo. Nearby, this casual udon (noodle) bar is the offshoot of Saint-Anne veteran Kunitoraya, although it can sometimes be harder to get a table here (no reservations are taken) than at the original. The corner space's exposed brick-and-iron design has Parisians declaring it 'très New York', though the experience is unequivocally Japanese: all simplicity, polite service and focus on the food. House-made udon comes cold for summer or with steaming bouillon in winter, and there are rice bowls topped with salmon and daikon, tempura, or katsudon (deep-fried pork cutlet) and umeboshi (pickled plums).

ELLSWORTH

34 rue de Richelieu
01 42 60 59 66
ellsworthparis.com
Open Mon 7–10pm, Tues–Sat
12.30–2.30pm & 7–10pm,
Sun 11.30am–3pm
Metro: Palais Royal–Musée du
Louvre, Pyramides

Ellsworth came into being as a casual little sibling for Verjus, though it quickly found its own dedicated following of expats, travellers and curious Parisians. While the kitchen sends out smart plays on American comfort food (fried chicken and spiced cabbage, rabbit-sausage corn dogs) and savvy international crowd pleasers (clams with harissa, lamb ragout with gnocchi and radicchio), the dining room is a surprisingly chic mix of sandstone and dimmed lights. Lunch and dinner are menu-based and small plates respectively, and both are attractively priced, especially so considering that absolutely everything is made in-house. The wine list features some natural wines, and mostly small producers. This is one of the most sought after brunch venues in Paris, so book ahead.

VERJUS & VERJUS BAR À VINS

52 rue de Richelieu (restaurant),
47 rue de Montpensier (bar)
01 42 97 54 40
verjusparis.com
Open Mon–Fri 7–11pm
(restaurant); Mon–Fri 6–11pm
(bar)
Metro: Bourse, Pyramides

A polished degustation dining experience this may be, but the dining room at Verjus, an evocative, decidedly romantic mix of big picture windows, white walls and vintage furniture, is far from stuffy and totally free from pretension. And, well, the food is not exactly French either, rather it's a stereotype-busting menu of stellar French produce, bold American moves and worldly sophistication, care of young chef-owners Braden Perkins and Laura Adrian. Downstairs, cellar bar Verjus Bar à Vins is, in fact, a cellar, with a suitably serious wine list and carefully prepared small plates. Just about everyone down here, including the staff, speaks English, but it all feels, somehow, fabulously and quintessentially Parisian.

13.

14.

Yasmine was born and raised in Paris. She studied fashion at the Studio Berçot in Paris and then moved to London where she worked for Vivienne Westwood for a number of years, designing the 'Red Label' collections. She is now part of the *Purple Fashion* magazine team and works as a stylist for various other publications. She recently launched her own lingerie line (*see* p. 004).

How would you define contemporary Parisian style

It's a 'négligé' look: effortless, red lips … Jeanne Damas [a French model] is the perfect Parisian.

What are your favourite pla to shop in the 1er?

The Palais Royal's shops (*see ma p. 001): Stella McCartney, Maiso Kitsuné (*see* p. 004) and Stéphan Chapelle's flower shop.

Where do you go for coffee?

Télescope (*see* p. 010) – it has the best coffee.

What is the best place for a night out?

The reopened Le Pompon club (*see map* p. 001), and cocktail bar Castel and nightclub Montana (*see map* p. 077).

Although Paris' smallest arrondissement is centred around the Bourse – the Palais Brongniart stock exchange – it's not *all* bankers and business suits. The growing fashion district of Étienne Marcel takes in its eponymous street, along with rue Montmartre, rue du Jour and rue Tiquetonne. It's a low-key area, usually uncrowded and full of young designers, streetwear and vintage shops.

Pedestrianised, food-focused rue Montorgueil is a convivial strip for those too grown-up for Canal Saint-Martin (*see* p. 130), while the old rag-trade district of Sentier is fast becoming tech start-up central, with a growing number of bars and restaurants catering to its young, digital crowd.

24   JUN 8016

SHOP
1 REPETTO (*see* map p. xiv)
2 ESPACE KILIWATCH
3 G. DETOU

EAT
4 LE SINOPLE

EAT AND DRINK
5 HERO

17

6 EDGAR
7 SATURNE
8 FRENCHIE BAR À VINS
9 LOCKWOOD
10 BACHAUMONT AND NIGHT FLIGHT

DRINK
11 SILENCIO

2E: BOURSE, ÉTIENNE MARCEL AND SENTIER

⊕ PASSAGE DES PANORAMAS

RUE SAINT-MARC

TO
REPETTO
(SEE MAP PAGE XIV)
←
✉

PLACE DE LA BOURSE

RUE DES JEÛNEURS

RUE DU SENTIER

RUE SAINT-FIACRE

La Comédie
des Boulevards

RUE NOTRE-DAME DE RECOUVRANCE

RUE POISSONNIÈRE

N

Palais
Brongniart

RUE MONTMARTRE

RUE NOTRE-DAME DES VICTOIRES

Bourse
🚇

2e

SILENCIO
●
🚻

RUE DU CROISSANT

RUE DES JEÛNEURS

RUE POISSONNIÈRE

SATURNE
●

RUE SAINT-JOSEPH

RUE DU SENTIER

RUE DE MULHOUSE

SENTIER

Théâtre
Montorgueil ■

RUE DE CLÉRY

**FRENCHIE
BAR À VINS**
●
🚻

RUE DES VICTOIRES

RUE PAUL LELONG

RUE RÉAUMUR

RUE MONTMARTRE

LOCKWOOD
●
🚇
Sentier

RUE DU NIL

RUE NOTRE-DAME

0   50 m

RUE DE CLÉRY

🚻

D'ABOUKIR

✉
Le Sentier
des Halles ■

RUE RÉAUMUR

RUE DES PETITS CARREAUX

TO
EDGAR,
LE SINOPLE
& HERO
(SEE MAP
LEFT)
→
🚻

RUE DU MAIL

RUE

RUE D'ABOUKIR

RUE LÉOPOLD BELLAN

RUE MONTORGUEIL

RUE DU LOUVRE

BACHAUMONT
& NIGHT FLIGHT
●

RUE D'ARGOUT

⊕

RUE MONTMARTRE

RUE BACHAUMONT

PLACE
DES
VICTOIRES

MATAMATA
COFFEE
BAR

RUE DE LA JUSSIENNE

RUE MANDAR

RUE GRENETA

Hôtel
des
Victoires

RUE

RUE HÉROLD

RUE ÉTIENNE MARCEL

ESPACE
KILIWATCH
●

G. DETOU
●

RUE MARIE STUART

Hôtel
Victoires
Opéra

RUE TIQUETONNE

RUE

✉

1er

RUE JEAN-JACQUES ROUSSEAU

RUE

RUE ÉTIENNE

Tour de
Jean-sans-Peur

RUE COQUILLIÈRE

RUE COQ HÉRON

LES
HALLES

RUE MONTMARTRE

RUE
MAUCONSEIL

RUE ÉTIENNE MARCEL

RUE DU BOULOI

RUE DU LOUVRE

E. DEHILLERIN
●
(SEE TEXT
PAGE 8)
🚻

Musée ■
du Barreau

RUE DU JOUR

Église
Saint-
Eustache

RUE DE TURBIGO

RUE MONDÉTOUR

RUE DU
COLONEL
DRIANT

🚻

RUE COQUILLIÈRE

Bourse de
Commerce

Jardin
Nelson Mandela

1.

REPETTO
22 rue de la Paix
01 44 71 83 12
repetto.fr
Open Mon–Sat 9.30am–7.30pm
Metro: Opéra

Anyone who's ever been to ballet classes will find it hard to walk past this pretty flagship shop. A dance-inspired fashion range of shoes, clothing and accessories is displayed alongside professional classical, jazz and tango shoes, leotards and tutus. The company's promise of 'grace and lightness' began when Rose Repetto created her first strong and supple ballet shoes for her dancer son, in a tiny workshop nearby. Yes, you'll no doubt feel a little pang when the perfectly postured ballerinas test their new satin pointes at the barre. But never fear: there's consolation waiting at l'Atelier Repetto, up the grand staircase, where you can create your own customised street-soled ballet flats, even if your own dance career ended at age eight.

ESPACE KILIWATCH

64 rue Tiquetonne
01 42 21 17 37
espacekiliwatch.fr
Open Mon 10.30am–7pm,
Tues–Sat 10.30am–7.30pm
Metro: Étienne Marcel, Sentier

Vintage clothes shopping in Paris can mean by-appointment dealers who trade in couture or designer pieces that sell for more than their contemporary counterparts. Kiliwatch, on the other hand, offers a more down-to-earth vintage experience. While you won't necessarily uncover any bargains, you will find a near overwhelming, but helpfully themed range of fripes (second-hand clothes), all in great condition. There's also new stock, including jeans, limited-edition sneakers, sunglasses, accessories and seasonal ranges – like French espadrilles in summer or toasty knits in winter – and a nicely curated magazine selection. Along with their staff, the very cool Alexandre Voisin and Jacques Grosz are a hoot and always happy to help.

3.

G. DETOU

58 rue Tiquetonne
01 42 36 54 67
Open Mon–Sat
8.30am–6.30pm
Metro: Étienne Marcel, Sentier

Although decidedly
unglamorous and primarily
aimed at professional chefs,
this old-fashioned food
store is for anyone who
looks upon travel as a way
to stock their pantry and/
or thinks food always makes
the best present. Selling a
phenomenal range of edible
cake decorations, chocolate,
essences, specialist flours,
and vanilla and tonka
beans, it also does as its
name suggests (G. Detou
is more a pun than a name:
j'ai de tout means 'I have
everything'). Either here
or in its next-door deli you
will, indeed, find practically
every type of edible thing
imaginable, including
supplies for the non-bakers
among us, like rare honey,
beautifully illustrated tinned
sardines, artisan mustard and
duck confit.

4.

LE SINOPLE

4bis rue Saint-Sauveur
01 40 26 69 66
lesinople.fr
Open Mon–Sat 7am–12am,
Sun 7am–6pm (kitchen
Mon–Sat 12–2.30pm &
7–10.30pm, Sun 12–2.30pm)
Metro: Sentier, Réaumur-
Sébastopol

There's a pleasant perversity
in escaping from rue
Montorgueil's feeding
frenzied crowds into the
discreet world of upmarket
sports club Klay. Workouts
are for members only, but
Klay's restaurant Le Sinople
happily receives guests.
There are two distinct spaces
to choose from. Outside is
a glass-ceilinged winter
garden of lush exotic plants,
where jaunty formica tables
are artfully (mis)matched
with velvet banquettes and
raffia chairs, care of designer
Charlotte Biltgen. Inside,
there's a smartly hard-edged
space filled with brass,
leather and marble, echoing
the sport club's historic
industrial architecture.
The menu is designed for
the fitness-minded, but,
apart from the four-egg-
white omelette, is far from
faddishly healthy.

Some of the city's best-preserved passages couverts – 19th-century arcades – can be found in the 2e. Passage Choiseul (*see map* p. 001) is considered the best preserved, Passage des Panoramas (*see map* p. 019) is full of vintage signage and Galerie Vivienne is possibly the prettiest of them all (*see map* p. 001).

5.

HERO

289 rue Saint-Denis
heroparis.com
Open Mon–Sat 12–2.30pm &
7–11pm, Sun 7–11pm
Metro: Strasbourg-Saint-Denis,
Bonne Nouvelle

Once known for a haughty resistance to global food trends, Parisians currently appear on a mission to embrace it all. And so we have this Korean street-food bar: an endearingly nutty, beautifully crafted hipster theme park spread over three floors. Feast on chef Haan Palcu-Chang's fried chicken, a great leveller where no-one can remain free of yangnyeom sauce (note the sink in the upstairs dining room), served with kimchi, pork buns and potato salad on the side. In the drinks department, there are shots of soju (a Korean rice spirit), an excellent range of Champagne by the bottle, or go to town on the absinthe-laced riff on bubble tea.

EDGAR
31 rue d'Alexandrie
01 40 41 05 69
edgarhotel.com
Open Mon–Sat
7.30–10.30am & 12–11pm, Sun
7.30–11am & 12–7pm
Metro: Strasbourg-Saint-Denis,
Sentier

In between a romantic, tree-lined square and the deliciously dishevelled passage du Caire, Guillaume Rouget-Luchaire has transformed one of Sentier's old garment workshops into a lively little hotel, with a downstairs bar and restaurant that draws locals as well as coddling the guests. A simple, mostly maritime menu – fresh oysters from Normandy, flash-grilled octopus, fried calamari – is served at lunch and dinner, and there's a genius-for-hangovers fish and chip brunch on Sundays. Tapas is also served daily from 3pm to 7pm. While the 12 stylishly eccentric guest rooms upstairs are designed by Rouget's artist, film director, set designer and photojournalist friends, it's his beautiful collection of Scandinavian mid-century pieces that fills the turquoise-walled restaurant and bar.

SATURNE

17 rue Notre-Dame des Victoires
01 42 60 31 90
saturne-paris.fr
Open Mon–Fri 12–2.30pm &
8–10.30pm
Metro: Bourse, Sentier

There's obviously a thrill in
the chase for 20-somethings
Sven Chartier and Ewen
Lemoigne, Saturne's chef and
sommelier respectively. Their
daily menus and natural wine
lists highlight rare and often
highly unusual ingredients –
ancient vegetables and
herbs, rare breeds of beef
or lamb, foraged seafood –
and many cult producers.
Set menus and well-chosen
wines by the glass relieve
what-to-choose stress, and
the Scandinavian simplicity
of the glass-roofed space is
also soothing, the restraint
enlivened by a few subtly
idiosyncratic Parisian touches
like the Serge Mouille wall
lights. Despite the quest for
novelty and on-trend kitchen
techniques, dishes have a
straightforward rusticity and
set new heights for the term
'produce driven'.

8.
FRENCHIE BAR À VINS
6 rue du Nil
01 40 39 96 19
frenchie-restaurant.com
Open Mon–Sun 7–11pm
Metro: Sentier, Réaumur-
Sébastopol

First up, let's address the
elephant in the room – or,
more precisely, the restaurant
across the way. Gregory
Marchand's Frenchie is
undeniably one of Paris'
finest neo-bistros, but it's
also tiny and near impossible
to book a table. What to do?
Head to Frenchie's wine bar
instead for a taste of what
all the fuss is about, without
the fuss. Here the high stools
and communal benches are
doled out first-come, first-
served, and many of the
sublimely inventive small
plates – skate wing salad,
various foamy riffs paired
with snow crab, pappardelle
with lamb ragout, elderflower
sorbet and almond crumble –
occasionally share menu
space with the restaurant.
A compelling wine list and
rather dishy staff on both
sides of the pass (hello,
open kitchen!) complete the
convivial experience. Come
early, and come often.

9.
LOCKWOOD
73 rue d'Aboukir
01 77 32 97 21
lockwoodparis.com
Open Mon–Sun 8am–2am
Metro: Sentier, Réaumur-
Sébastopol

This happy hipster clubhouse
is another fine venture
by brothers Olivier and
Christophe Lehoux, who
also had a hand in Silencio
(see p. 030) and Sydney bars
Pocket, Button and Stitch.
Start the day with macchiatos
(made with brother Thomas'
Belleville Brûlerie beans)
on a street-facing log, and
end it with cocktails in the
flickering candlelight of
the sandstone basement.
In between, head here
for Brooklyn-meets-Bondi
daytime dining or an Italian
aperitivo hour with plentiful
snacks, good Italian wines
and even better Negronis.
The crowd is international,
though it's also a favourite
hang of local hospitality types
who obviously appreciate
its all-day and most-of-the-
night hours.

8.

8.

8.

9.

9.

BACHAUMONT AND NIGHT FLIGHT

18 rue Bachaumont
01 81 66 47 50 (restaurant),
01 48 58 56 23 (bar)
hotelbachaumont.com
Open Mon–Sun 12–3pm &
7–11pm (restaurant); Mon–Sun
5pm–2am (bar)
Metro: Sentier, Étienne Marcel

The booming but hotel-starved 2e has finally got a destination hotel in the Bachaumont. With its restaurant and Night Flight bar care of Experimental Group – the trio responsible for the Experimental Cocktail Club in the 1er, the Prescription Cocktail Club in the 6e (*see* p. 087) and SoPi's Grand Pigalle Hotel Bar (*see* p. 124) – it's definitely not just a place to stay. Highly regarded interior designer Dorothée Meilichzon has a penchant for pattern: her plum-toned marble-printed textiles pop against the sober navy and grey of the restaurant's classical interior. Joyfully light-filled by day and candlelit at night, come here for brasserie favourites like slow-cooked lamb or prime rib with purée (mashed potato). Night Flight is a wood and velvet mood piece with the Experimental cocktail kings working their magic, and DJs and live sets creating the mood.

SILENCIO

142 rue Montmartre
01 40 13 12 33
silencio-club.com
Open Tues–Thurs 6pm–4am,
Fri–Sat 6pm–6am (non-members
after midnight)
Metro: Bourse, Grands
Boulevards

Subterranean by several flights of stairs, film director David Lynch's private club won't deliver *Mulholland Drive*'s multilingual illusionists or *Twin Peaks*–style dancing dwarves. What you will find is an adult theme park (no, not one of those) that's open to non-members after midnight, sometimes before if the bouncers like the look of you. It hosts film screenings, talks and live concerts early in the evening before DJs crank it up. The cocktails flow, and there's some occasional Parisian dirty dancing and lots of pretty people, but the big enchantment is the decor, from black-on-black toilets to tunnels of gilt mandalas, all designed to the 'nth' degree by Lynch himself.

RUE DE TURBIGO

RUE AU MAIRE

3e

RUE DES GRAVILLIERS

404

DERRIERE

TO
MAP RIGHT
(VIA RUE DES GRAVILLIERS
& RUE PASTOURELLE)

Lebenson
Gallery
Zürcher

in)(between
Gallery

RUE

CHAPON

The ancient neighbourhood of the Marais straddles the 3e and 4e, and the border between the two is obscured by one of the city's densest shopping strips. Every French fashion label you'll want to blow your luggage allowance on – A.P.C., Bensimon, Isabel Marant and so on – has at least one shop in either rue des Francs-Bourgeois or rue Vieille-du-Temple, and these are joined by loads of individual boutiques.

This is also a wonderful place to simply stroll around. Heading north to the Place de la République, the once-sleepy streets of the Haut ('high') Marais, including boulevard Beaumarchais and boulevard des Filles du Calvaire, are now home to Paris' coolest shops, bars and restaurants, along with some of the city's best contemporary galleries.

24   JUN 80T6

SHOP
1 BONTON
2 BENSIMON HOME AUTOUR
   DU MONDE
3 YVON LAMBERT BOOKSHOP
4 PAPIER TIGRE
5 OFR
6 COMMUNE DE PARIS 1871
7 QUIDAM DE REVEL

17

SHOP AND EAT
8 MARCHÉ DES ENFANTS
   ROUGES
SHOP, EAT AND DRINK
9 MERCI
10 LA MAISON PLISSON
EAT
11 FRAGMENTS

3E: MARAIS AND
HAUT-MARAIS

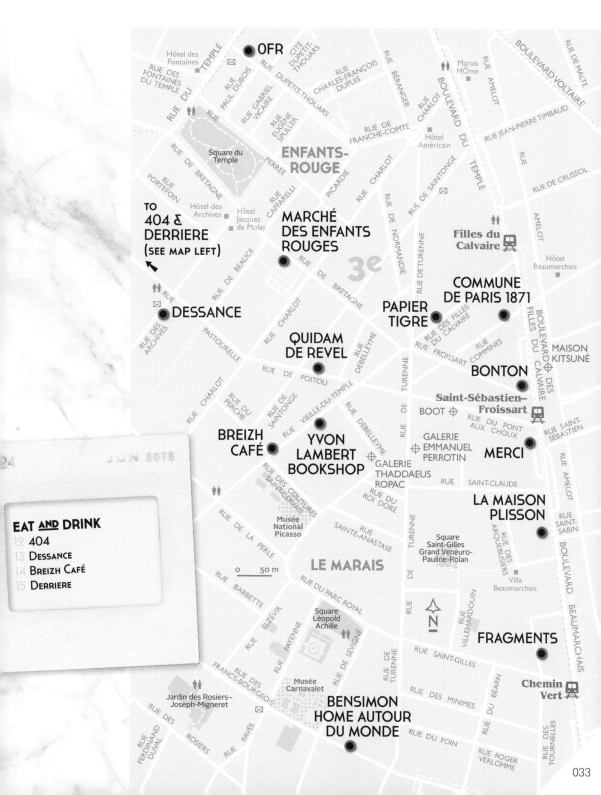

OFR

Hôtel des
Fontaines

CITÉ
DUPETIT-
THOUARS

Marais
HÔme

BOULEVARD VOLTAIRE

RUE DE MALTE

RUE DES
FONTAINES
DU TEMPLE

RUE
PAUL DUBOIS

RUE DUPETIT-THOUARS

RUE
CHARLES-FRANÇOIS
DUPUIS

RUE BÉRANGER

RUE
AMELOT

RUE DU TEMPLE

RUE
GABRIEL
VICAIRE

RUE
EUGÈNE
SPULLER

RUE DE
FRANCHE-COMTÉ

RUE
CHARLOT

BOULEVARD DU TEMPLE

RUE JEAN-PIERRE TIMBAUD

Square du
Temple

PERRÉE

ENFANTS-
ROUGE

Hôtel
Américain

RUE DE SAINTONGE

RUE
RUE DE CRUSSOL

RUE DE BRETAGNE

PICARDIE

RUE
CHARLOT

RUE
PORTEFOIN

Hôtel des
Archives

Hôtel
Jacques
de Molay

MARCHÉ
DES ENFANTS
ROUGES

RUE DE NORMANDIE

Hôtel
Beaumarchais

TO
**404 &
DERRIERE**
(SEE MAP LEFT)

RUE DE BEAUCE

RUE
CAFFARELLI

RUE DE BRETAGNE

3e

RUE DETURENNE

Filles du
Calvaire

RUE
AMELOT

DESSANCE

RUE DES
ARCHIVES

PASTOURELLE

RUE
CHARLOT

COMMUNE
DE PARIS 1871

BOULEVARD DES FILLES DU CALVAIRE

MAISON
KITSUNÉ

PAPIER
TIGRE

RUE DES FILLES
DU CALVAIRE

RUE FROISSART

RUE
COMMINES

QUIDAM
DE REVEL

RUE DE POITOU

RUE DEBELLEYME

RUE DE TURENNE

BONTON

RUE
CHARLOT

RUE DU
PERCHE

RUE DE
SAINTONGE

VIEILLE-DU-TEMPLE

RUE DEBELLEYME

Saint-Sébastien–
Froissart

BOOT

RUE DU PONT
AUX CHOUX

RUE SAINT-
SÉBASTIEN

BREIZH
CAFÉ

YVON
LAMBERT
BOOKSHOP

GALERIE
EMMANUEL
PERROTIN

MERCI

RUE DES COUTURES
SAINT-GERVAIS

GALERIE
THADDAEUS
ROPAC

RUE DU
ROI DORÉ

RUE
SAINT-CLAUDE

LA MAISON
PLISSON

RUE
SAINT-SABIN

Musée
National
Picasso

RUE DE LA PERLE

RUE
SAINTE-ANASTASE

LE MARAIS

RUE DE TURENNE

Square
Saint-Gilles
Grand Veneuro-
Pauline-Rolan

RUE DES
ARQUEBUSIERS

BOULEVARD

0   50 m

RUE BARBETTE

RUE DU PARC ROYAL

Villa
Beaumarchais

BEAUMARCHAIS

RUE
ELZÉVIR

RUE
PAYENNE

Square
Léopold
Achille

RUE DE SÉVIGNÉ

N

RUE
VILLEHARDOUIN

FRAGMENTS

RUE DE
TURENNE

RUE SAINT-GILLES

Chemin
Vert

RUE
FRANCS-BOURGEOIS

Musée
Carnavalet

RUE DES MINIMES

RUE DU BÉARN

Jardin des Rosiers–
Joseph-Migneret

RUE DES
ROSIERS

RUE
PAVÉE

BENSIMON
HOME AUTOUR
DU MONDE

RUE DU FOIN

RUE ROGER
VERLOMME

RUE DES
TOURNELLES

RUE
FERDINAND
DUVAL

RUE
DES

JUN 8016

24

033

1.

BONTON

5 boulevard des Filles du Calvaire
01 42 72 34 69
bonton.fr
Open Mon–Sat 10am–7pm
Metro: Saint-Sébastien-Froissart

Irène Cohen, from the visionary retail family behind Merci (*see* p. 044) and children's label Bonpoint, wanted to create a family destination rather than just a shop. Indeed, Bonton, her rambling three-floor emporium, feels like a celebration of childhood itself. Shelves and baskets brim with beautiful toys, party things, kids' bracelets and necklaces, jewel-coloured bed linen and little people's cookware. There's even a photo booth and children's hairdresser. Then there's the relaxed, playful clothes, from newborn to size 12, which come in rich, earthy toned cotton, linen and wool – they are so wearable and so delightful that parents have been known to shed a tear when their littlest finally outgrows the range.

2.

BENSIMON HOME AUTOUR DU MONDE

8 rue des Francs-Bourgeois
01 42 77 06 08
bensimon.com
Open Mon–Sat 11am–7pm,
Sun 1.30–7pm
Metro: Chemin Vert

Le tennis Bensimon, the coloured canvas plimsoll synonymous with casual French style, was launched in 1978, and its creators, the two brothers Bensimon, have gone on to become one of France's creative powerhouses, working the signature artful insouciance of these shoes into a total lifestyle. Their original Marais homewares shop carries a covetable collection of objects and furniture sourced from international designers and artists, all displayed alongside their iconic, indispensible shoes, as well as jackets, shirts, shifts and chinos. If you're in need of a style boost, the ever-elegant Charlotte Bensimon, wife of co-founder Serge, is often in store to advise. For an even more sharply distilled version of Serge Bensimon's aesthetic, head to **Gallery S. Bensimon**, just around the corner at 111 rue de Turenne.

3

YVON LAMBERT BOOKSHOP

108 rue Vieille-du-Temple
01 42 71 89 05
shop.yvon-lambert.com
Open Tues–Sat 10am–7pm,
Sun 2–7pm
Metro: Filles du Calvaire,
Rambuteau

Legendary art-world figure Yvon Lambert opened his Collection Lambert gallery in Avignon in 2000. This northern 'outpost' combines a small gallery space with a bookshop jam-packed with art books (including rare and out-of-print editions), posters, DVDs, CDs, T-shirts and art objects. Limited editions by the likes of visual artists such as David Shrigley, Roni Horn and Douglas Gordon line the walls and can be surprisingly affordable; their exhibition catalogues and artists' edition books are also fantastically collectible. The little box of a gallery space punches above its weight with some extraordinary shows and spill-out-onto-the-street openings.

4.

PAPIER TIGRE
5 rue des Filles du Calvaire
01 48 04 00 21
papiertigre.fr
Open Tues–Fri 11.30am–7pm,
Sat 11am–8pm
Metro: Filles du Calvaire

Papier Tigre's collection of notebooks, postcards, calendars, lettersets and decorations are oh-so-tactile, bright and geometric, and combine a French flair for the typographic with a clean Japanese and Scandinavian sensibility. Out the back of the bright, plywood shopfront, you can glimpse the design process at work; the everyday goings-on of the studio are testament to the company's made-in-France ethos. The pretty paper goods are joined by other Parisian wares, such as Macon & Lesquoy's sweet and witty embroidery brooches, clips and patches, the locally made men's skincare line Le Baigneur, and Kerzon's candles inspired, amongst other things, by Paris' Parc des Buttes Chaumont's woody slopes.

5.

OFR
20 rue Dupetit-Thouars
ofrsystem.com
Open Mon–Sat 10am–8pm,
Sun 2–7pm
Metro: Temple

Brother and sister team Alexandre and Marie Thumerelle have been selling the city's most interesting collection of printed matter for almost two decades at this bookshop-cum-gallery, which feels more akin to a neighbourhood drop-in centre than a retail space. Locals pop in for the twice-weekly openings, book launches and other events, while casual passers-by are lured in by the stacks of art and architecture books, packed magazine stands and a beautiful jumble of artisanal accessories and homewares. Beware: losing an afternoon here is not uncommon, even before you've discovered the back-room gallery, which exhibits both local and international artists' work.

COMMUNE DE PARIS 1871
19 rue Commines
09 81 90 13 37
communedeparis1871.fr
Open Mon–Sat 10.30am–7pm
Metro: Saint-Sébastien-Froissart

- -

Alexandre Maïsetti and Sébastien Lyky created their menswear label as a cheeky homage to one of Paris' lesser known historical periods: the glory days of the Paris Commune, the city's most revolutionary government ever. Drop by this mosaic-floored former butcher's shop for T-shirts emblazoned with provocative '70s-style motifs care of Paris' best illustrators, or classically tailored shirts and suiting that keep the revolutionary references subtle with tricolour buttons or piping. A candle specially created for the store by Astier de Villatte (*see* p. 002) emits spicy whiffs of citrus and nutmeg, conjuring the hazy, heady past of the 19th-century radicals, painters and poets who once manned the commune barricades.

QUIDAM DE REVEL

26 rue de Poitou
01 42 71 37 07
Open Tues–Sat 2–7.30pm
Metro: Saint-Sébastien-Froissart

Antiquarian Philippe Harros and his art historian partner Emmanuelle Chesnel have been a source of by-appointment-only beautiful vintage clothing for costume designers, stylists, fashion houses and canny Parisians over in the 10e for almost two decades. This glittering little shop houses their couture jewellery collection. Most of the pieces are from iconic design houses – Lanvin, Schiaparelli, Yves Saint Laurent – and are museum-quality. Bold, gold '80s chokers face off with '60s haut-hippy silver, while drawers secret a cache of 18th- and 19th-century pieces, rare Scandinavian work and exquisite items by cult Parisian designers Claude Lalanne and 'the poet of metals' Line Vautrin.

MARCHÉ DES ENFANTS ROUGES

39 rue de Bretagne
Open Tues–Thurs 8.30am–1pm & 4–7.30pm, Fri–Sat 8.30am–1pm & 4–8pm, Sun 8.30am–2pm
Metro: Temple

At almost 400 years old, this covered market is the oldest in Paris (its poetic name harks back even further, to the days when an orphanage occupied the site and its little charges were clad in red). Haut-Marais locals stock up on flowers and fresh produce here, but Enfants Rouges' real attraction is its varied food stalls: try an Afro-Antillean curry with accra (fish fritters), a Moroccan tagine or an all-organic roast and vegetable gratin plate. Postprandial browsing at Fabien Breuvart's vintage photography shop (on rue Charlot) or the occasional brocante stalls on rue de Bretagne is all part of the ritual too.

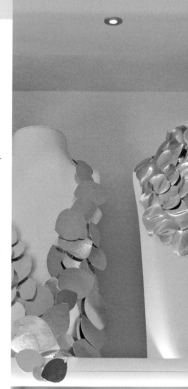

PARIS TIP

Right in the thick of the Marais' shopping frenzy, two stunning 16th-century hôtels house the Musée Carnavalet, a wonderful museum that documents Paris' history and everyday life, from pre-Roman Gaul to the present day.

9.

MERCI

111 boulevard Beaumarchais
01 42 77 00 33
merci-merci.com
Open Mon–Sat 10am–7pm
Metro: Saint-Sébastien-Froissart

Whether it's your first or 31st visit to cult concept shop Merci, there's always a heart-fluttering moment when you glimpse the vintage Fiat 500 mascot guarding the courtyard entrance. That's because you're just moments away from Paris' most seductive collection of designer picks, house-label basics, accessories, jewellery, homewares, furniture, linen and stationery. Once inside, first take in the fruits of Merci's latest thematic collaborations (anything from knickers made with recycled Italian silk to artisanal cleaning products) filling the dramatic entrance, then it's up, down and around the sprawling three floors of this former wallpaper factory. Hungry? Salads, cake and organic wine await in the cinema café, the library or garden-facing **La Cantine**.

LA MAISON PLISSON
93 boulevard Beaumarchais
01 71 18 19 09
lamaisonplisson.com
Open Mon–Sat 8.30am–9pm,
Sun 8.30am–5pm
Metro: Chemin Vert

Delphine Plisson, former CEO
of the Claudie Pierlot fashion
label, created this gourmet
épicerie (delicatessen) with
the needs of Marais locals
in mind – somewhere to
pick up a wedge of artisan
cheese and some radishes
or raspberries on the way
home from work. But its
wonderful selection of regional
French products is a delight
for visitors too. Produce is
grouped together in mini-
departments, from wine and
chocolate to charcuterie
and rotisserie chickens, all
manned by welcoming, expert
and charming staff. Despite
the shop's size, you'll find
shopping here an intimate
affair. When you're all stocked
up, head to the marble and
rattan neo-bistro next door
for some healthy, hearty
mains or a killer riz au lait
(rice pudding).

FRAGMENTS
76 rue des Tournelles
Open Mon–Sun 8.30am–
4.30pm
Metro: Chemin Vert

You'll be tempted to order a takeaway coffee and head to the Place des Vosges' lawns just around the corner, but it'd be a shame not to linger in Fragment's inky interior or loll on a stool out on the street. The ever welcoming Youssef Louanjli has created an evocative space in a former stables, where exposed brick walls, ironwork and Bruce Lee posters are teamed with wonderfully aged wooden furniture. The barista team turns out excellent espresso on a vintage Mirage machine from Coutume (*see* p. 100), with beans from Belleville Brûlerie and Danish Coffee Collective. They also do aeropress, filter and a mean iced coffee. Coffee partners, like madeleines and canelles (moulded cakes with custard centres), are fresh and fragrant, while tartines (open sandwiches), savoury tarts and some antipodean brunch favourites like avocado smash or eggs on toast emerge from a little open kitchen.

PARI/ TIP
The Marais is home to Paris' densest concentration of contemporary art spaces. Stellar international artists show at galeries Emmanuel Perrotin (Sophie Calle, Maurizio Cattelan; *see map* p. 033), Thaddaeus Ropac (Gilbert & George, Anselm Kiefer; *see map* p. 033) and Marian Goodman (Chantal Akerman, Annette Messager; *see map* p. 055).

12.

404

69 rue des Gravilliers
01 42 74 57 81
404-resto.com
Open Mon–Fri 12–2.30pm
& 7.30–11.30pm, Sat & Sun
12–4pm & 7.30–11.30pm
Metro: Arts et Métiers

Set in one of the oldest
private houses in Paris,
404 was a revelation when
it opened in 1990, giving
North African food, normally
associated with budget
holes-in-the-wall or home
cooking, a rock'n'roll edge.
Two and a half decades on,
Algerian-Parisian-Londoner
Mourad Mazouz' first hit
restaurant is as intoxicating
as ever. The old Marais bones
of stone and exposed beams
mix it up with Berber-licious
leather, brass and wood
decor, while the kitchen
delivers a menu of fresh but
authentic Maghrebi dishes:
think fragrant tagines, brik
pastries stuffed with prawns,
and herbed and charred
sardines. These tasty dishes
don't come cheap, but
they're beautifully executed,
well spiced and use top-
quality ingredients.

13.

DESSANCE

74 rue des Archives
01 42 77 23 62
dessance.fr
Open Wed–Sun 12–11pm
Metro: Arts et Métiers

The 'tout sucré' degustation
at this dessert-only
restaurant not only lets you
eat dessert first, but also
second, third, fourth and
fifth. If that idea makes
your teeth ache, there's
an intriguing salé/sucré
option too. With this menu,
Christophe Boucher's stellar
pastry chef credentials are
tweaked and twisted to
create small, not necessarily
sweet, dishes that combine
herbs, vegetables, fruits and
spices in an explosion of
colour, flavour and texture.
Or visit the warm, woody and
rather sexy space for a single
(yes, sweet) course in the
afternoon, along with a plate
of mignardises (petits fours)
with a coffee, herbal infusion,
fruit elixir or whisky shot.

14.

BREIZH CAFÉ

109 rue Vieille-du-Temple
01 42 72 13 77
breizhcafe.com
Open Wed–Sun 11.30am–
10.30pm
Metro: Filles du Calvaire,
Rambuteau

Procuring a table at this little
bit of Brittany slap in the
mid-Marais can require some
planning or much patience,
but book or queue if you can.
This corner crêperie turns out
perfect galettes de blé noir:
thin, earthily savoury, crispy-
edged buckwheat crepes
which are a Breton speciality.
Fillings include the standard
ham, gruyere and sunny-
side-up egg alongside more
unusual ingredients like –
sea asparagus, artichokes,
smoked duck breast. There's
an extensive artisan cider
menu and, most surprisingly
of all, beautifully toned and
textured Japanese takes on
the traditional Breton cider
jugs and bowls, care of the
owner's Japanese ceramicist
wife. After you've had your
fill of crepes, pop next door to
their épicerie (delicatessen)
for some cult Bordier butter
and yoghurt and other Breton
treats to take away.

DERRIERE
69 rue des Gravilliers
01 44 61 91 95
derriere-resto.com
Open Mon–Sun 12–2.30pm &
4–11.30pm
Metro: Arts et Métiers

What was possibly once the most over-hyped restaurant in Paris, Derriere – yes, it does mean 'arse' – has settled nicely into comfortable second-gen coolness. Its interior is a grab bag collection of fabulous 20th-century furniture, along with a ping-pong table and a stray motorcycle; upstairs a warren of rooms gives the impression you've stumbled into someone's apartment (and someone quite fabulous at that). Come for a peek at the fabulous interior and a spot of people-watching, and you'll undoubtedly return for the romantic courtyard tables, the French-classics-meet-international-favourites menu or an after-dinner whisky at all-grown-up front bar, **Andy Wahloo**.

Antoine, a former architect, is the founder and design director of branding, identity and architecture studio Be-Poles. His identity work includes the Pompidou Centre, New York's NoMad Hotel, L'Occitane, Merci (*see* p. 044) and La Maison Plisson (*see* p. 046). Be-Poles also publishes a photographic travel series, *Portraits de Villes*.

Where do you find inspiration?

I find inspiration looking at the sky above Paris. Our office is on the 9th floor in front of Beaubourg (what we Parisians call the Pompidou) and the view from there is really inspiring. I live in Montmartre and I have a view over Paris there too. I need to look at the city from above – these moments make me feel free.

For everyday inspiration in the Marais, go to 0Fr (*see* p. 040), an amazing bookshop and art gallery. Those guys – Alex and Marie – have SO MUCH energy.

What are your favourite Marais shops?

The best shop ever is Merci, a rare selection of cool things and beautiful installations. The team there is nice and the kitchen is really good too. Go to La Cantine downstairs and ask for Sylvie. Also, just down the road, there's La Maison Plisson. Delphine

Plisson selects all the products for quality and taste, which makes the place special.

What is the best place for a night out?

Sorry, but the best night out is not in the Marais – it's in Pigalle! L'Isolé on rue Frochot (*see map* p. 114) has good music and great cocktails. The graphic design of the identity is also so original.

Where do you go to escape?

I'm a road-bike rider. The best feeling is when I go for a Saturday morning ride with my mates. We ride 130km west of Paris, to a place called the Vallée de Chevreuse. It's a national park and just a little bit south-west of Versailles. We pass castles and beautiful old houses, and stop in at Rambouillet for a coffee at the market place. We feel so lucky when we get back to Paris after our green expedition.

This densely populated, fabulously pretty part of the lower Marais has much of its medieval layout still intact. It has long been the home to Paris' Jewish population and, in later times, its gay community, it's now also a shopping mecca, with department store BHV and big French chains staking out rue de Rivoli. Here too is Hôtel de Ville, home to the city government since 1357.

Hard to miss is the Centre Pompidou, home to the Musée National d'Art Moderne, Europe's largest modern art museum. Across the Pont Notre-Dame and Pont Marie lie, respectively, the fabulously photogenic Seine islands, Île de la Cité – with its famous Cathédrale Notre-Dame de Paris – and Île Saint-Louis.

24   JUN 8016

SHOP
1 AU PETIT BONHEUR LA CHANCE
2 MARIAGE FRÈRES

17

EAT
3 L'AS DU FALLAFEL
4 BERTHILLON
EAT AND DRINK
5 BENOIT

4E: MARAIS, HÔTEL DE VILLE, ÎLE DE LA CITÉ AND ÎLE SAINT-LOUIS

1.

AU PETIT BONHEUR LA CHANCE

13 rue St Paul, Village St Paul
01 42 74 36 38
aupetitbonheurlachance.fr
Open Mon–Sat 11am–1pm &
2.30–6.30pm
Metro: Sully-Morland, Saint-Paul

In this shop full of childhood memories and domestic detail, owner Maria-Pia Varnier brings together a cache of forgotten treasures that even those who grew up far from France will be able to appreciate. Shelves upon shelves are full of the things you hope to chance upon at a country brocante market but never quite do: stacks of illustrated '70s children's books, pochoir (stencilled) café au lait bowls, enamel house numbers, real French milk bottles, buttons, bath toys and pre-war school supplies – the list goes on. As someone else has done all the hunting hard yards for you, don't expect a bargain, but do come ready for cute overload.

2.

MARIAGE FRÈRES

30 rue du Bourg-Tibourg
01 42 72 28 11
mariagefreres.com
Open Mon–Sun
10.30am–7.30pm
Metro: Hôtel de Ville

This original tea emporium honours the tea trading Mariage brothers' deep roots in the Marais by way of a touching small museum. Take the stairs to see its collection of pots, cups and canisters, as well as documents and photographs that so beautifully conjure the world of 19th-century trade. The company's smart black-and-yellow caddies are ever ready to purchase, but the adventure really starts if you wander into the headily fragranced traditional loose-leaf-tea room, with its wooden counters and a few thousand teas to choose from. If you've hit a busy time, head across the road to the associated mini-shop, where you can also buy canisters or choose porcelain cups or a pot in peace.

PARIS TIP

The Maison Européenne de la Photographie is one of the world's best contemporary photography museums. Temporary exhibitions have included the likes of Jacques Henri Lartigue, Annie Leibovitz and William Klein.

3.

L'AS DU FALLAFEL

32–34 rue des Rosiers
01 48 87 63 60
Open Mon–Thurs & Sat–Sun
11am–12am
Metro: Saint-Paul

This part of the Marais is known as the Pletzl ('little place' in Yiddish), and has been the heart of Jewish Paris for over 600 years. Despite the gentrification of the surrounding streets, it still has its kosher bakers and butchers, and, in rue des Rosiers, its jostling falafel joints. The jury is forever out on which falafel place is best, but for sheer Sephardic theatre, you can't beat L'As ('The Ace'). Come early or be prepared to queue, and note: this busy strip is one of the few places in Paris where scoffing food on the street won't attract withering stares from passing Parisians. Make the most of it!

BERTHILLON
29–31 rue Saint-Louis en l'Île
01 43 54 31 61
berthillon.fr
Open Wed–Sun 10am–8pm
Metro: Pont Marie, Saint-Paul

This legendary Île Saint-Louis ice-cream shop got experimental with its flavours five or so decades before the current more-is-more ice-cream moment and remains both highly inventive and ever the purist. Knockout flavours include agenaise (Armagnac and prunes), lavender, and salted caramel, while the seasonal range might turn up a haunting tonka-bean base shot through with dark chocolate shards in winter, or a crisp lemon-thyme sorbet for spring. You can get a Berthillon boule (ball or scoop) elsewhere, but there's nothing like marking the crossing of the Seine with a pilgrimage to this shop. Sit in or be prepared to queue, and get ready for every flavour to become your new favourite.

5.

BENOIT

20 rue Saint-Martin
01 58 00 22 05
benoit-paris.com
Open Mon–Sun 12–2pm &
7.30–10pm
Metro: Châtelet, Hôtel de Ville

In the early 20th century, Les Halles was Paris' biggest produce market, and nearby restaurant Benoit kept the market's butchers' and greengrocers' stomachs full. Today, Les Halles is a shopping mall, and these streets are full of tourists rather than market traders, but Benoit has retained its bygone bistro magic. The restaurant's original family owners entrusted their iconic place to superstar chef Alain Ducasse ten years ago and all the traditional bistro trappings remain – waistcoated waiters, mirrors, red velvet – along with its big bold flavours, slow braises, and dark, rich sauces, not to mention fruit tarts and booze-sloshed cakes.

Tariq Krim was born and raised in the 4e and, a few stints in San Francisco aside, has lived in Paris all his life. He is a serial entrepreneur and founded innovative French tech companies Netvibes and Jolicloud. He is also a journalist who explores digital life, the 'slow world' and contemporary culture. He can be found writing in Paris' best coffee places.

How would you define Paris right now?

A vibrant city that is finally opening up to the world, while also preserving what makes it unique.

Where do you find inspiration?

I love walking in the small streets and sitting down in cafés. I love sitting in Place des Vosges or Palais Royal and listening to music while writing.

What are your favourite places/things to do in the 4e?

Spending time on the Île Saint-Louis and having a sorbet at Berthillon (*see* p. 059), still the best in the world in my opinion. And Hôtel de Sens (*see map* p. 055) – the cutest mini-castle in town.

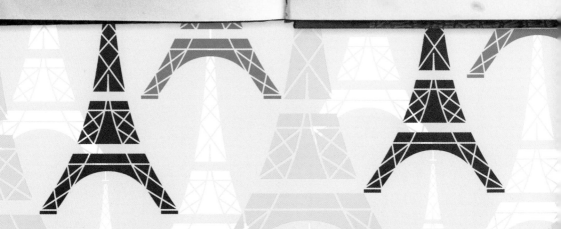

Where do you go for coffee?

Two places I love are Fragments (*see* p. 047) and Boot (*see map* p. 033), a tiny shoe place that serves damn good coffee.

What is the best place for a night out?

Drinks at Lockwood (*see* p. 028) and then a quick dance at Silencio (*see* p. 030).

Where do you go to escape?

A quick hop to Normandy is always good: fresh air, good food and cider, and still time to catch the last train to return to Paris on a Sunday night.

This is Paris' oldest neighbourhood – apart from the Île de la Cité – the Romans built here in the 1st century BC, although the Latin of its name reflects the language of choice at its medieval universities. Yes, it's been a student precinct for centuries, and while the 5e's raffish and radical days are long gone, its Sorbonne university ensures it's still got enough brainy insouciance to keep things interesting.

It seems fitting to pay your respects at the Panthéon, a church turned secular mausoleum where writers Voltaire, Hugo and Zola are buried. The Jardin des Plantes, with its splendid green stretches, is also perfect for thinking and reflecting. Away from the tourist zones, new bars, cafés and bistros are constantly springing up.

24   JUN 80T6

SHOP
1. Shakespeare & Company
2. Diptyque
3. Le Bonbon au Palais

EAT
4. Coutume Instituutti
5. La Grande Mosquée de Paris Restaurant

EAT AND DRINK
6. Restaurant AT & Bar à Vin
7. Café de la Nouvelle Mairie

5E:
LATIN QUARTER

Pont
Marie

QUAI DU
MARCHE NEUF

ÎLE DE
LA CITÉ

RUE CHANOINESSE

QUAI AUX FLEURS

VOIE GEORGES POMPIDOU

PONT
LOUIS-PHILIPPE

La Seine

RUE SÉGUIER

Saint-Michel
Notre-Dame

Saint-
Michel

SHAKESPEARE
& COMPANY

Cathédrale
Notre-Dame
de Paris

QUAI DE BOURBON

Hôtel Saint-
Louis en l'Isle

QUAI SAINT-LOUIS EN L'ÎLE

RUE DANTON

BOULEVARD SAINT-MICHEL

METAMORPHOSES

RUE DE LA HARPE

RUE SAINT-JACQUES

Square
René Viviani

Square
Jean
XXIII

QUAI DE MONTEBELLO

Square
de l'Île
de France

Hôtel des
Deux Iles

ÎLE
SAINT-LOUIS

BOULEVARD

PONT DE
L'ARCHEVÊCHÉ

QUAI D'ORLÉANS

La Seine

PONT DE LA
TOURNELLE

Cluny–
La Sorbonne

Square
de Cluny

RUE LAGRANGE

SAINT-GERMAIN

RUE DES BERNARDINS

QUAI DE LA TOURNELLE

COUTUME
INSTITUUTTI

Maubert
Mutualité

DIPTYQUE

RESTAURANT AT
& BAR À VIN

BOULEVARD
SAINT-GERMAIN

RUE DE LA SORBONNE

RUE

DES

ÉCOLES

le M.
Saint-
Germain

Hôtel
Atmosphères

RUE SAINT-VICTOR

RUE DE POISSY

RUE DU CARDINAL LEMOINE

RUE DES FOSSÉS SAINT-BERNARD

QUARTIER
LATIN

BOULEVARD SAINT-MICHEL

RUE CHAMPOLLION

RUE SAINT-JACQUES

Square Paul
Langevin

RUE MONGE

RUE DES ÉCOLES

N

RUE VALETTE

RUE CUJAS

RUE SOUFFLOT

PLACE DU
PANTHÉON

LE BONBON
AU PALAIS

RUE DU CARDINAL LEMOINE

RUE JUSSIEU

Collection des
Minéraux-
Jussieu

5e

Panthéon

RUE CLOVIS

Cardinal
Lemoine

JUSSIEU

RUE LINNÉ

Jussieu

RUE JUSSIEU

RUE SAINT-JACQUES

Les
Dames du
Panthéon

Hôtel des
Grands
Hommes

RUE CLOTILDE

RUE DESCARTES

RUE DU CARDINAL LEMOINE

RUE MONGE

Square
des Arènes
de Lutèce

RUE CUVIER

CAFÉ DE LA
NOUVELLE
MAIRIE

RUE THOUIN

Jardin
des
Plantes

RUE PIERRE ET
MARIE CURIE

Hôtel
Gay-Lussac

Chapelle
Saint-Patrick

RUE DULM

RUE LHOMOND

RUE TOURNEFORT

RUE MOUFFETARD

RUE LACÉPÈDE

RUE
SAINT-MÉDARD

RUE LACÉPÈDE

Best
Western

RUE DE QUATREFAGES

La
Galerie
des Enfants

Relais
Saint-
Jacques

RUE AMYOT

Place
Monge

RUE GEOFFROY

Comfort
Hotel

RUE ERASME

RUE DULM

Cour
aux
Ernest

VAL-DE-GLÂCE

RUE DU POT DE FER

RUE
ORTOLAN

LA GRANDE
MOSQUÉE DE PARIS
RESTAURANT

RUE DES FEUILLANTINES

RUE GAY-LUSSAC

Cour
Pasteur

RUE RATAUD

RUE LHOMOND

RUE DE MIRBEL

RUE DAUBENTON

RUE CENSIER

RUE SAINT-HILAIRE

Église
Val-de-Grâce

RUE VAUQUELIN

RUE LAGARDE

Censier–
Daubenton

RUE DE SANTEUIL

Musée du
Service de
Santé des
Armées

RUE CLAUDE BERNARD

Square
Saint-
Médard

RUE DE LA CLEF

RUE DES FOSSÉS SAINT-MARCEL

BERTHOLLET

RUE DE
L'ARBALÈTE

0   1 km

RUE BROCA

RUE PASCAL

RUE MONGE

RUE DU FER A MOULIN

Square
Théodore
Monod

RUE VESALE

RUE DES FOSSÉS SAINT-MARCEL

RUE SCIPION

BOULEVARD DE PORT-ROYAL

PÂTISSERIE
SADAHARU
AOKI

Le Seven

SHAKESPEARE & COMPANY
37 rue de la Bûcherie
01 43 25 40 93
shakespeareandcompany.com
Open Mon–Sun 10am–11pm
Metro: Saint-Michel, Cluny–La
Sorbonne

George Whitman, Paris' great expat literary patron and friend to writers like Allen Ginsberg and Jack Kerouac, bequeathed his Left Bank English-language bookshop to daughter Sylvia after his death in 2011. Apart from some gentle modernisation, it remains the rich, rambling, bohemian hub that's nurtured, nourished and often housed writers and readers since the Beat era. Mythological back story aside, there are books to be browsed and bought here. The thoughtfully curated section on Paris – including history, food, politics and city life – should be your first stop, followed by the endless shelves of fiction where you'll find every novel you've ever wanted to read. Don't miss the antiquarian collection next door too; with its first editions by the likes of D.H. Lawrence and James Joyce, as well as more affordable treasures. It's a bibliophile's delight.

DIPTYQUE

34 boulevard Saint-Germain
01 43 26 77 44
diptyqueparis.fr
Open Mon–Sat 10am–7pm
Metro: Maubert-Mutualité,
Cardinal Lemoine

In the world of perfume houses, 'flagship' is synonymous with doorman-fronted flash mini-cities, but not so at Diptyque. Its headquarters, housed in the original shop, are decidedly intimate, with eclectic carpet, wallpaper, painted finishes and objects all honouring founders Christiane Gautrot, Desmond Knox-Leet and Yves Coueslant's spirit of creative curiosity and sensory wonder. The full range of perfumes, home fragrances and skincare is here, including the label's commemorative Collection 34, named for the shop and fittingly elegant *and* intriguing. Even the complimentary gift wrapping is a flight of fancy, using a riot of rainbow tissue paper in surprising, joyful combinations.

3.

LE BONBON AU PALAIS

19 rue Monge
01 78 56 15 72
bonbonsaupalais.fr
Open Tues–Sat 11am–7pm
Metro: Maubert-Mutualité,
Cardinal Lemoine

This 'palace of sweets' is a tour of the tastes and smells of childhood for its French customers – everything in the shop comes from traditional confiseur (confectioner) workshops all over France. Affable owner Georges Marques had a lifelong desire to open such a place and he understands the tender nostalgia his wares summon. The shop's schoolroom decor adds to the feel of bygone times, as do the apothecary jars filled with treats like cocoa-dusted pralines, crystallised flowers, caramels and pâtes de fruit (fruit jellies). If overwhelm sets in and you just can't decide what to try, the pretty pastel guimauve – fragrant, soft marshmallow blocks from Bayonne in south-western France – are the best you'll find in Paris.

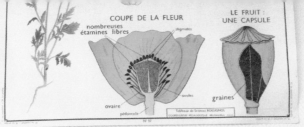

CARTES
BANCAIRES
MINIMUM 10€

PARIS TIP

Not far from the historic Grande Mosquée (*see* p. 070) is the Jean Nouvel–designed Institut du Monde Arabe, a fabulous piece of modern architecture that houses a fascinating collection of art and objects from the Arabic-speaking world, as well as an observation deck.

4.

COUTUME INSTITUUTTI

33 rue du Sommerard (main
entrance 60 rue des Écoles)
01 40 51 89 09
institut-finlandais.fr
Open Tues–Sat 9am–6pm,
Sun 10am–6pm
Metro: Cluny–La Sorbonne,
Odéon

Finns love to tell you they
consume the most coffee
per capita in the world, and
here, tucked away inside
the Finnish Institute's Paris
headquarters, they've built
a shrine to the Finnish
coffee break to prove it.
Coutume (*see* p. 100), the
veteran café-roastery from
the 7e, runs the place, with
endearingly enthusiastic
baristas turning out a rapid
stream of flat whites and long
blacks to elegantly unharried
students who manage to
make university life look like
a Nordic fashion shoot. The
lofty space is all pale wood
and utilitarian grace – perfect
for scoffing cardamom buns
and cheesecake or settling in
with smoked-salmon-stuffed
rye sandwiches.

5.

LA GRANDE MOSQUÉE DE PARIS RESTAURANT

39 rue Geoffroy-Saint-Hilaire
01 43 31 14 32
restaurantauxportesdelorient.com
Open Mon–Sun 9am–12am
Metro: Saint-Marcel, Place
Monge

Whether you're here to
see Paris' beautiful early-
20th-century mosque and
its sculpted arcades that
recall the Alhambra in
Granada, or you're in need of
refreshments after too many
hours at the nearby Jardin
des Plantes' museums, the
moment you enter this walled
enclave, the fragrance of thé
à la menthe will transport you
straight to Tangier or Tunis.
Tree-shaded courtyards give
way to jewel-coloured rooms
that in turn give way to tiled
inner courtyards. While away
an afternoon or evening with
either the aforementioned
mint tea or superbly sweet-
sour citronade (homemade
lemonade) and nutty pastries,
or fill up on tagines and
couscous at lunch or dinner.

4.

4.

5.

5.

5.

5.

RESTAURANT AT & BAR À VIN

4 rue du Cardinal Lemoine
01 56 81 94 08 (restaurant),
01 42 01 20 49 (bar)
atsushitanaka.com
Open Tues–Sat 12.15–2pm &
8–9.30pm (restaurant);
Wed–Sun 7pm–2am (bar)
Metro: Pont Marie, Cardinal
Lemoine, Jussieu

Atsushi Tanaka is one of a number of young, ambitious Japanese chefs who've opened their own Parisian place after time in the city's Michelin-starred kitchens. In the shadow of grand dining dinosaur Tour d'Argent, Tanaka's space is fiercely art school to d'Argent's fusty haute couture, its austere Zen ruptured by a neo-expressionist mural on one wall and colourful deconstructed wooden sculptures on the other. The lengthy dinner degustation requires commitment, but a shorter and very affordable lunch menu delivers a beautiful smattering of Tanaka's stage-set-like plates, each evoking magical places: broccoli, leaves and vegetal dust evoke a forest floor, while baby whelks bob in a Jerusalem artichoke foam as if still by the seashore. The adjoining bar is a hospitality favourite, where the Paris cheffy mafia comes to drink from the all-natural wine list and eat charcuterie into the wee hours.

CAFÉ DE LA NOUVELLE MAIRIE

19 rue des Fossés Saint-Jacques
01 44 07 04 41
Open Mon–Fri 8am–12am
Metro: Place Monge,
Cardinal Lemoine

Just by the Panthéon and overlooking the Place de l'Estrapade fountain, this neighbourhood favourite pushes all the classic Paris-bistro buttons. Staff, in their cordial, non-committal way, are reassuringly, well, Parisian. Look beyond the vintage signage and dark-wood chairs and you'll see a keen mid-20th-century eye behind many of the pieces strewn about. Look again and you'll notice the blackboard of well-priced wines by the glass are mostly natural and all from small estates (if you're feeling serious about tasting, go straight to the huge list, which features multiple vintages from favourite vignerons). Food too is straightforward and comforting (terrines, foie gras, sausages in lentils, clafoutis) but nicely finessed, and the coffee is faultless but not fussed over.

PARIS TIP

The Marché Mouffetard might be Paris' most photogenic produce market, but it can be suffocatingly crawling with tourists. Instead, head to the close by but far calmer Place Monge on Wednesday, Friday and Saturday mornings.

Sylvia was born in Paris, attended university in London and Edinburgh, and returned to Paris in her early 20s. She has been the proprietor of Shakespeare & Company (*see* p. 066) since 2006, after taking up the reins from her father, George Whitman, who founded the bookstore in 1951.

How would you define contemporary Parisian style?

I don't know what it is, but Clémence Poésy [a French actress] has it.

What are some must-read books about Paris?

Julian Green's *Paris* – each chapter reads like a beautiful portrait of a secret corner of the city – and Elaine Dundy's *The Dud Avocado*. I just want to join [Dundy's character] Sally Jay Gorce on one of her chaotic, hilarious and frankly bizarre days in bohemian Paris.

What's your favourite shop?

Metamorphoses (*see map* p. 065), a small, dark jewellery store in the 5th run by a woman who is tiny and has been there for 50 years. I want to write a tale about this place, where you disappear into a dark world when you put on the wrong ring.

What are the city's best bookish attractions?

Shakespeare & Company, obviously! And walking along the river, browsing the bouquinistes [second-hand book stalls]. The Luxembourg Gardens is a stunning place to read a book and walk in the footsteps of many great writers. I read one of Milan Kundera's books for the first time sitting by the lovers' fountain here; it's one of my best memories.

Where do you go for coffee?

The Coutume Instituutti café (*see* p. 070) – finally, some good coffee and a relaxed ambience in what has become a touristy quartier!

Where do you go to escape?

A day trip to the forest of Fontainebleau, or, if I can't leave the city, Père Lachaise [cemetery].

A byword for bohemian for much of the last century, the haunt of Jean-Paul Sartre and Simone de Beauvoir, and the scene of street fighting and barricades during the student demonstrations and general strike of May 1968, Saint-Germain-des-Prés is today better known for its chic shopping and priceless people-watching. Antique shops, big, beautiful, luxury-label flagships and scores of artisans line the neighbourhood's streets.

Legendary cafés like Les Deux Magots and Café de Flore draw armies of tourists, while still somehow managing to keep their elegant, bookish old-timers, and Le Jardin du Luxembourg in the south of the precinct is a green, serene piece of Parisian paradise.

24   JUN 8016

SHOP
1 HERMÈS
2 BULY 1803
3 ASSOULINE
4 ATELIER FLORENCE LOPEZ
5 MARIE-HÉLÈNE DE TAILLAC
6 GALERIE SALON
7 PÂTISSERIE SADAHARU AOKI

EAT AND DRINK
8 AUX PRÉS
9 SEMILLA

DRINK
10 PRESCRIPTION COCKTAIL CLUB

6E: SAINT-GERMAIN-DES-PRÉS

N

DRIES VAN NOTEN
Square Honoré Champion

BULY 1803

6e

La Seine

QUAI DE CONTI

Institute de France

Square Gabriel Pierné

Monnaie de Paris

RUE DE SEINE

QUAI DE CONTI

0   50 m

RUE BONAPARTE

RUE DES BEAUX-ARTS

L'Hôtel

RUE JACOB

RUE

RUE VISCONTI

RUE DE SEINE

RUE MAZARINE

RUE GUÉNÉGAUD

Galerie Da-End

Galerie Forêt Verte

RUE DE NEVERS

Galerie Aethiopia

Théatre Galerie de Nesle

SAINT-GERMAIN-DES-PRÉS

RUE SAINT-BENOÎT

Hôtel Saint-Germain-des-Prés

RUE BONAPARTE

RUE

JACOB

RUE JACQUES CALLOT

RUE DE NESLE

L'ECUME DES PAGES

Hôtel Bel Ami

ASSOULINE

MUSÉE NATIONAL EUGÈNE DELACROIX

PRESCRIPTION COCKTAIL CLUB

RUE DAUPHINE

MONTANA

Square Laurent Prache

RUE DE L'ABBAYE

RUE DE FURSTENBERG

RUE DE L'ÉCHAUDÉ

SEMILLA

RUE MAZARINE

RUE ANDRÉ MAZET

CAFE DE FLORE

PLACE SAINT-GERMAIN-DES-PRÉS

Église de Saint-Germaine-des-Pres

RUE DE BUCI

Hôtel Le Régent

LES DEUX MAGOTS

RUE DE RENNES

BOULEVARD

Square Félix Desruelles

GALERIE SALON

RUE DE BUCI

RUE DE SEINE

RUE GRÉGOIRE DE TOURS

RUE DE L'ANCIENNE COMÉDIE

RUE SAINT-ANDRÉ DES ARTS

SAINT-GERMAIN

Saint-Germain-des-Prés

TO AUX PRÉS, HERMÈS & PÂTISSERIE SADAHARU AOKI
(SEE MAP LEFT)

RUE DU FOUR

RUE PRINCESSE

RUE DE MONTFAUCON

BOULEVARD

SAINT-GERMAIN

Mabillon

RUE CLÉMENT

Odéon

RUE DE SEINE

RUE GRÉGOIRE DE TOURS

RUE DE CONDÉ

RUE MONSIEUR LE PRINCE

RUE DES CANETTES

RUE GUISARDE

Musée-Librairie du Compagnonnage

Auditorium Saint-Germain

CASTEL

MABILLON

RUE LOBINEAU

RUE DES QUATRE-VENTS
Louis II

RUE DES QUATRE-VENTS

RUE BONAPARTE

RUE

PLACE SAINT-SULPICE

SAINT-SULPICE

RUE SAINT-SULPICE

RUE DE CONDÉ

RUE DE L'ODÉON

RUE CASIMIR DELAVIGNE

Fontaine Saint-Sulpice

Église Saint-Sulpice

RUE PALATINE

RUE GARANCIÈRE

RUE
SAINT-SULPICE

RUE DE TOURNON

MARIE-HÉLÈNE DE TAILLAC

PLACE   SAINT-SULPICE

RUE SERVANDONI

077

1.

HERMÈS

17 rue de Sèvres
01 42 22 80 83
hermes.com
Open Mon–Sat 10.30am–7pm
Metro: Sèvres-Babylone,
Saint-Sulpice

The original Hermès boutique over the river may have notched up well over a century (the founder's son, Charles-Émile Hermès, began retailing the company's fine leather saddles there in 1880), but the august brand's most recent incarnation – opened in 2010 – has a historic back story all of its own. Set in the former Lutetia swimming pool, a listed Art Deco lovely from 1935, original, sinuous iron balconies outline each floor of this extraordinary luxury goods superstore, while totally 21st-century wooden pods rise up almost ten metres from what was once the pool floor. Signature scarves, bags, belts, shoes, books and, yes, equestrian accoutrements are displayed within, against a shimmering backdrop of original glass mosaics. It's dazzling.

BULY 1803
6 rue Bonaparte
01 43 29 02 50
buly1803.com
Open Mon 11am–7pm,
Tues–Sat 10am–7pm
Metro: Saint-Germain-des-Prés

This tantalisingly timeworn skincare and fragrance shop dates back only as far as 2014, but its cherry wood panelling, brass taps, velvet drapes and rustic terracotta tiles are a convincing period confection indeed. Ramdane Touhami (formerly behind candle maker Cire Trudon) and his wife Victoire de Taillac-Touhami's extensive range includes oils, incense, clays, waters, pomades, powders and milks, along with exquisite artisan-made brushes and combs. Inspired by the apothecary trade across history and cocooned in wistfully nostalgic packaging, all products are in fact produced with the most advanced contemporary knowledge, with new-tech formulations all being paraben-, alcohol- and silicon-free.

3.

ASSOULINE

35 rue Bonaparte
01 43 29 23 20
assouline.com
Open Mon–Sat
10.30am–7.30pm
Metro: Saint-Germain-des-Prés

Martine and Prosper Assouline's global publishing empire is a paean to the big, beautiful coffee table book and a luxury lifestyle brand for bibliophiles. In this seductive red-walled boutique, the original, their glossy, glamorous titles on fashion, art, architecture, photography, design and travel fill floor-to-ceiling bookshelves. There's also a collection of very pick-me-up-and-stroke-me library and desk accessories, bookishly themed candles and special edition Goyard trunks. Everything comes gift-wrapped and blobbed with a red wax seal and can either be stashed in one of their fetching, fabulously load-bearing canvas totes or, if you're taking it luxe all the way, a book bag made from embossed leather.

4.

ATELIER FLORENCE LOPEZ

rue du Dragon
06 60 44 33 75
florencelopez.com
Open by appointment
Metro: Saint-Germain-des-Prés,
Saint-Sulpice

While there's a great amount of pleasure to be had stumbling around French brocante markets hoping for a pulse-quickening find, a far more, well, Parisian way to source antique and vintage pieces is to engage an expert. Antiquarian and interior designer Florence Lopez has one of the most sought after eyes in the business, with a who's who of haute-bourgeoisie and cool-kid clients (just between you and me, these *might* include actor and musician Charlotte Gainsbourg and one of the Daft Punk duo). Her studio, where she presents her seasonal collections, is an airy 1920s atelier daubed in her signature hues of deep green, blue and grey. If you're in the market for extraordinary 20th-century pieces, from vases, mirrors, sculptures and prints to sofas and sideboards, visits are by appointment.

PARIS TIP

Over two decades after his death, the home of Serge Gainsbourg remains shuttered and empty, and has become an impromptu, graffiti-daubed shrine to the adored Parisian musician and lover of Brigitte Bardot and Jane Birkin. Pay your insouciant respects at 5bis rue de Verneuil (*see map p. 091*).

5.

MARIE-HÉLÈNE DE TAILLAC
8 rue de Tournon
01 44 27 07 07
mariehelenedetaillac.com
Open Mon–Sat 11am–7pm
Metro: Odéon, Mabillon

There's a bohemian ease to the work of jeweller Marie-Hélène de Taillac: precious and semiprecious stones shine in her unassuming, storybook-simple designs, the radiance and rainbow colours of the gems allowed full reign. With walls of summer sky blue, poppy-red sofas and pearl-like spherical pendant lights dropping from a lofty ceiling, her Tom Dixon–designed boutique is as luminous and joyful as her collections. The pretty, witty charms on silk cords are affordable, while the rings, neckpieces and drop earrings are, despite their seductive simplicity, no mere playthings (the iconic Pucci-tribute neckpiece and cabochon ring are part of the permanent collection of the Musée des Arts Décoratifs de Paris).

GALERIE SALON

4 rue de Bourbon le Château
01 44 27 00 81
galeriesalon.fr
Open Mon–Sat 11am–7pm
Metro: Mabillon, Saint-Germain-
des-Prés

- -

This delightful bijou shop
packs in all the now-ness that
you might encounter in one
of the city's famed concept
superstores, along with a
good splash of beauty and
wonder that's the preserve of
the neighbourhood's antique
dealers. Young antiquarians
Carole and Stéphane
Borraz earned their stripes
specialising in Swedish and
Italian pieces at the Marché
aux Puces de Saint-Ouen
(*see* p. 201). Their penchant
for the rustic, intimate and
curious now also sees them
working with contemporary
makers such as Astier de
Villatte (*see* p. 002), Berlin
potter Kühn Keramik, crochet
and knit queen Sophie Digard
and A Paris Chez Antoinette
Poisson, a hand-printed
wallpaper specialist.

7.

PÂTISSERIE SADAHARU AOKI

35 rue de Vaugirard
01 45 44 48 90
sadaharuaoki.com
Open Tues–Sat 11am–7pm,
Sun 10am–6pm
Metro: Saint-Sulpice,
Luxembourg

Unless you've been in a silent order or stuck in solitary confinement for the last ten years, it would be hard to have missed the macaron fever that swept first Paris and then the world. Maven and maverick macaron stores Ladurée and Pierre Hermé still draw the crowds, but there's also a third way: Japanese pâtissier Sadaharu Aoki. Come to his sparse, modern shop by the Jardin du Luxembourg and grab a box of his signature flavours of matcha (green tea), sesame and wasabi. Or pick up one of his blissfully fragrant, viridian-green, matcha-almond croissants. There's another boutique over at 56 boulevard de Port-Royal (*see map* p. 065), where you can sit in with a pot of tea and indulgence of choice.

8.

AUX PRÉS

27 rue du Dragon
01 45 48 29 68
restaurantauxpres.com
Open Mon–Sun 12–2.30pm
& 7–11pm
Metro: Saint-Germain-des-Prés,
Sèvres-Babylone

Legendary Left Bank restaurant Claude Sainlouis, where 'le tout Paris' came to see and be seen in the 1950s and '60s, has been reborn as Aux Prés. The ambitious but unassuming TV chef Cyril Lignac has retained the best of the mid-century decor – an enveloping assortment of marble, dark floral wallpaper, vintage leather bar stools and booth seating – and presents a similarly nostalgic menu of bistro favourites (foie gras, steak and purée, strawberries and cream) with some fresh, globally roaming flourishes (candied cod with black miso, peas and bacon). Set menus are good value for a neighbourhood that tends towards style over substance. The jaunty cocktail list seems totally in sync with the decor and you can't go past the Germanopratin – cucumber, lemon juice, gin, St-Germain elderflower liqueur and Champagne.

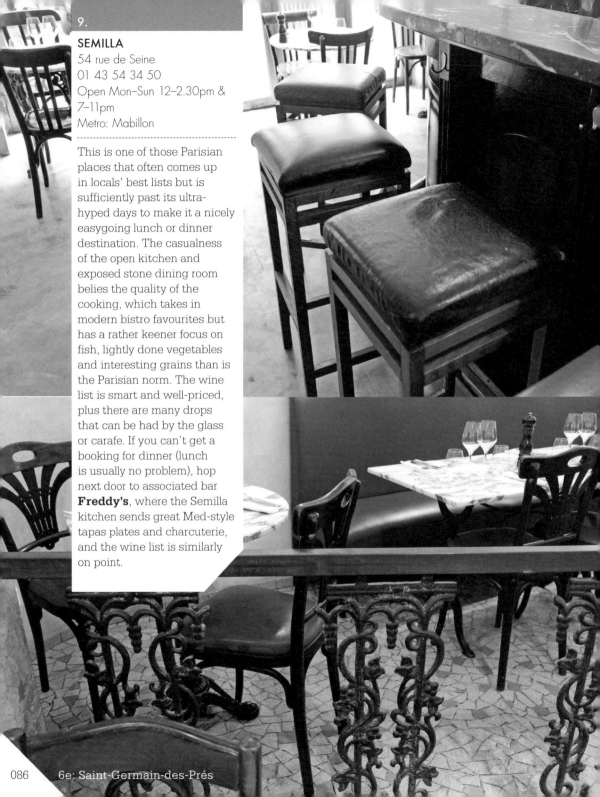

SEMILLA

54 rue de Seine
01 43 54 34 50
Open Mon–Sun 12–2.30pm &
7–11pm
Metro: Mabillon

This is one of those Parisian places that often comes up in locals' best lists but is sufficiently past its ultra-hyped days to make it a nicely easygoing lunch or dinner destination. The casualness of the open kitchen and exposed stone dining room belies the quality of the cooking, which takes in modern bistro favourites but has a rather keener focus on fish, lightly done vegetables and interesting grains than is the Parisian norm. The wine list is smart and well-priced, plus there are many drops that can be had by the glass or carafe. If you can't get a booking for dinner (lunch is usually no problem), hop next door to associated bar **Freddy's**, where the Semilla kitchen sends great Med-style tapas plates and charcuterie, and the wine list is similarly on point.

PRESCRIPTION COCKTAIL CLUB
23 rue Mazarine
09 50 35 72 87
prescriptioncocktailclub.com
Open Mon–Thurs & Sun
7pm–2am, Fri–Sat 7pm–4am
Metro: Saint-Michel

You don't have to have a late-night bacchanal planned to come here (though one might eventuate anyway). A Prescription cocktail can turn a post-shopping apéro into a celebration or can be the perfect wake-up if you've had an afternoon of one too many museums. The Cocktail Club's founders Romée de Goriainoff, Olivier Bon and Pierre-Charles Cros have been spreading the mixology love across Paris, London and Ibiza for the last ten years, but this remains a singularly cosy and atmospheric spot, with gorgeous speakeasy decor (including a secret room), a drinks' list full of interesting tipples and a crowd worth watching.

Florence Lopez is an antiquarian, interior designer and visionary 'scenographer' with projects in Paris, London, Berlin, Venice, New York, Chicago and Los Angeles. At her Saint-Germain-des-Prés antique store (*see* p. 080), she specialises in rare pieces from the 20th century. Another speciality is contemporary artist collaborations. Her work has been featured in *Architectural Digest*, *Casa Vogue*, *The World of Interiors* and *Elle Decor*.

How would you define contemporary Parisian style?

Fondation Louis Vuitton by Frank Gehry (even if he is an American architect!) – a great sculpture in our very Parisian Bois de Boulogne [garden].

What are some of the iconic but less visited places to go in the 6e?

I so like the former artists' studios, which are now fondations or musées dedicated to their particular artist, like Delacroix, Dubuffet and Zadkine. Some also have marvellous fragrant gardens, where you can find a place to be in peace.

What are the best shopping, coffee and nightlife venues near your studio?

I love vintage, so I don't shop a lot, but I do like visiting these beautiful shops: Dries Van Noten (a Belgian fashion label; *see map* p. 077) and Marie-Hélène de Taillac (*see* p. 082). For coffee, I'd choose Café de Flore (*see map* p. 077), but very early, at 7.30am! And at night, the Montana nightclub (*see map* p. 077), as it's decorated by Vincent Darré, or Aux Prés (*see* p. 084) for cocktails and dinner at the bar.

What keeps you living and working where you do?

The 6e is a village, full of surprises, and still full of inspiring and lively characters. I do regret the loss of the great bookshops, although we still have L'Ecume des Pages (*see map* p. 077). I love all the intense cultural activity of the galleries and antique shops around rue de Seine and rue Bonaparte, plus the Café de Flore and Les Deux Magots (*see map* p. 077). And, of course, there is nothing more beautiful than an early morning walk along the Seine.

Aristocratic to the core and flush with hôtels particuliers (grand townhouses) to prove it, this is a precinct of Michelin-starred restaurants and luxury shopping. Apart from stalking famous resident Karl Lagerfeld and seeking out empire-bolstering monuments, you'll probably find yourself in the 'faubourg' – as the 7e is often called, after Faubourg Saint-Germain – either to eat, shop or for that most Parisian of sights, the Eiffel Tower.

The 7e is also home to three of Paris' most iconic museums – the impressionist-filled Musée d'Orsay, the Musée Rodin, housed in the sculptor's former house and studio, and the stylish, sensual but highly controversial Jean Nouvel–designed Musée du quai Branly, featuring indigenous art.

24   JUN 8076

SHOP
1 Le Bon Marché
2 India Mahdavi Petits Objets

SHOP, EAT AND DRINK
3 La Grande Épicerie de Paris

17

EAT AND DRINK
4 L'Arpege
5 L'Atelier Saint-Germain de Joël Robuchon
6 Clover
7 Rosa Bonheur Sur Seine
8 Coutume

7E: EIFFEL TOWER AND FAUBOURG SAINT-GERMAIN

COURS LA REINE

COURS LA REINE

ROSA BONHEUR SUR SEINE

QUAI D'ORSAY

PONT DE LA CONCORDE

Fontaine des Mers

Concorde

PLACE DE LA CONCORDE

Bassin Octogonal

Musée de l'Orangerie

QUAI DES TUILERIES

Jardin des Tuileries

Renaissance Paris Vendôme Hotel

RUE DE RIVOLI

RUE D'ALGER

RUE DU 29 JUILLET

Tuileries

Grand Bassin Rond

VOIE GEORGES POMPIDOU

AVENUE DU GÉNÉRAL LEMONNIER

RUE ROBERT ESNAULT-PELTERIE

Palais Bourbon

La Seine

QUAI ANATOLE FRANCE

QUAI AIMÉ CÉSAIRE

Invalides

RUE DE L'UNIVERSITÉ

ARISTIDE BRIAND

INVALIDES

RUE DE LILLE

Musée d'Orsay

Musée d'Orsay

QUAI VOLTAIRE

PONT ROYAL

RUE SAINT-DOMINIQUE

Assemblée Nationale

BOULEVARD

RUE DE SOLFÉRINO

RUE DE BELLECHASSE

RUE DE LILLE

RUE DE POITIERS

RUE DE VERNEUIL

RUE DU BAC

RUE DE BEAUNE

RUE DE CONSTANTINE

RUE DE BOURGOGNE

RUE DE MARTIGNAC

RUE CASIMIR PÉRIER

RUE LAS CASES

RUE SAINT-DOMINIQUE

Solférino

SAINT-GERMAIN

RUE DE VILLERSEXEL

L'ATELIER SAINT-GERMAIN DE JOËL ROBUCHON

SERGE GAINSBOURG HOUSE

Varenne

RUE DE

RUE DE BOURGOGNE

CITÉ MARTIGNAC

INDIA MAHDAVI PETITS OBJETS

GRENELLE

RUE DE BELLECHASSE

RUE DE SAINT-SIMON

Deyrolle

RUE DU BAC

RUE DU PRÉ AUX CLERCS

Académie Hotel

L'ARPEGE

7e

RUE DE GRENELLE

Rue du Bac

BOULEVARD

CLOVER

Musée Rodin

RUE DE VARENNE

RUE SAINT-GUILLAUME

RUE DE GRENELLE

SAINT-GERMAIN

RUE DES SAINTS-PÈRES

BOULEVARD DES INVALIDES

CITÉ VANEAU

RUE VANEAU

CITÉ DE VARENNE

Musée Maillol

BOULEVARD RASPAIL

RUE DE LA CHAISE

Square Roger-Stéphane

Théâtre Saint-Germain

RUE BARBET DE JOUY

RUE DE LA PLANCHE

RUE DE SÈVRES

Le Centaure

Saint-François-Xavier

RUE DE BABYLONE

COUTUME

RUE DE BABYLONE

RUE DU BAC

Square des Missions Étrangères

Square Boucicaut

Le Petit Chomel

RUE CHOMEL

Sèvres-Babylone

RUE MONSIEUR

RUE OUDINOT

RUE

RUE VANEAU

LA GRAND ÉPICERIE DE PARIS

RUE DU BAC

LE BON MARCHÉ

RUE DE SÈVRES

RUE SAINT-PLACIDE

RUE DUPIN

BOULEVARD RASPAIL

Saint-Sulpice

RUE DU CHERCHE-MIDI

6e

BOULEVARD DES INVALIDES

RUE PIERRE LEROUX

RUE ROUSSELET

Vaneau

RUE DE

RUE DU CHERCHE-MIDI

RUE DU REGARD

RUE D'ASSAS

RUE DE RENNES

RUE CASSETTE

Rennes

0   200 m

1.

LE BON MARCHÉ

24 rue de Sèvres
01 44 39 80 00
lebonmarche.com
Open Mon–Wed & Sat
10am–8pm, Thurs–Fri
10am–9pm
Metro: Sèvres-Babylone

Spare yourself the tour buses of the Grands Boulevards and make a beeline to quintessential Parisian department store Le Bon Marché instead. Louis-Charles Boileau and Gustave Eiffel designed, it was launched in 1852 to be 'a new kind of store that would thrill all the senses'. The current interior is the work of superstar designer Andrée Putman, whose 1984 glamourous remodel seems even more in fashion today than it did back then. And, yes, from the vast perfume section and marvellous menswear to big-name luxury labels such as Lanvin and Dior to Parisian it-girl go-tos like Majestic and Carven, count on retail thrills aplenty.

2

INDIA MAHDAVI
PETITS OBJETS
19 rue Las Cases
01 45 55 88 88
india-mahdavi.com
Open Mon–Sat 11am–7pm
Metro: Assemblée Nationale,
Solférino

Iranian-born, Paris-based interior designer India Mahdavi has a way with detail and colour and it's beautifully on display in this shop of 'little things'. Here her line of playful, vibrant homewares has its own dedicated space (her furniture showroom is down the street at 3 rue Las Cases, her studio is next door to that). Window displays are a riot of voluptuous oranges, earthy mustards, dark chocolates and sweet sea greens, while further inside the store the colour fest continues with lampshades, graphic cushions, sculptural stools and Provençal-style ceramics. Mahdavi's stylish jumble also includes Mongolian cashmere throws and other objects sourced from various artisans around the world.

3.
LA GRANDE ÉPICERIE DE PARIS

38 rue de Sèvres
01 44 39 81 00
lagrandeepicerie.com
Open Mon–Sat 8.30am–9pm
Metro: Sèvres-Babylone

The one-time 'food counter' at Le Bon Marché (*see* p. 092) has evolved over the last century into La Grande Épicerie de Paris, a vast, upmarket grocery-store-cum-gastronomic-spectacle. Housed on the lower floors of one of Le Bon Marché's vast buildings, four main departments cover 'basic, traditional, rare and ultra-sophisticated' groceries, some 30,000 of them. Expect jams from Jura, hand-harvested Camargue salt and Provence's finest olive oil, along with well-sourced seasonal fresh produce and over 2000 wines in a basement cellar. House kitchens stock patisserie, chocolaterie and boulangerie (bakery) counters, as well as provide picnic or hotel-room-ready dishes. French kitchen fantasies can be fulfilled in the cookware department, or retire to the light-filled, leafy atrium of **La Table de la Grande Épicerie** for a reviving glass of Ruinart Champagne. If you've really gone to town, have your purchases delivered or take advantage of the taxi reservation service.

4.
L'ARPEGE

84 rue de Varenne
01 47 05 09 06
alain-passard.com
Open Mon–Fri 12–2.30pm & 7–10.30pm
Metro: Varenne, Rue du Bac

The relative merit of Paris' numerous two- and three-Michelin-star restaurants is always a hot topic. With even lunch a substantial investment and bookings hard to secure, choosing a fine-dining venue can be as hard work as earning the euros to eat there. Alain Passard's three-star L'Arpege might lack the palace hotel trappings and theatrical pretence of many of its peers, but it stands out for a few reasons: firstly, Passard's focus on vegetables; secondly, the service has an informal warmth; and thirdly, there's a lunch menu that will give you change from €200 per person if you go easy on the wine. For that you get an opportunity to weigh in on the 'is it worth it?' controversy and an 11-course degustation, a gently paced journey of dishes like beetroot tartare with horseradish cream, oeuf à la coque (Passard's take on the boiled egg) and fish fresh from the Breton coast teamed with foraged wild sorrel.

4.

PARIS TIP

A neighbourhood
market with
a staggering
view of the
Eiffel Tower, the
Saxe-Breteuil
on the place
de Breteuil sells
deliciously fresh
produce and
beautiful flowers.

3.

4.

5.

L'ATELIER SAINT-GERMAIN DE JOËL ROBUCHON

5 rue Montalembert
01 42 22 56 56
atelier-robuchon-saint-germain.com
Open Mon–Sun 11.30am–
3.30pm & 6.30pm–12am
Metro: Solférino, Rue du Bac

Joël Robuchon may be a global franchise as much as a chef these days, but this is his original 'atelier'. With its red-leather stools arranged around an open kitchen, the 40-seat Pierre-Yves Rochon–designed space is pure Paris before the hipster apocalypse: dark, posh and pervy. Here Robuchon pioneered the concept of casual fine dining, and while his degustation menus of small plates may not offer up any surprises, dishes like lobster carpaccio or foie gras–stuffed quail will delight with the quality of produce and intensity of flavour. Bookings are only accepted for the 11.30am and 6.30pm sittings (and these need to be made several weeks in advance). After these times, join the queues for one of the few spontaneous fine-dining opportunities to be had in Paris.

6.

CLOVER
5 rue Perronet
01 75 50 00 05
clover-paris.com
Open Tues–Sat 12–2.30pm &
7.30–10pm
Metro: Saint-Germain-des-Prés,
Mabillon, Rue du Bac

Although this is a favoured
haunt of the well shod and
well-heeled, Clover's tiny,
corridor space is so intimate,
so cheery and the food so
nourishing and comely, it's
the opposite of intimidating.
Jean-François Piège, a
Michelin-starred chef, opened
Clover with wife Elodie to
explore his 'cuisine instinctif',
a move towards the healthy
and sustainable. Food is,
however, far from austere,
with forays into the earthy
side of the French country
kitchen – say wild-duck-filled
pastries – while keeping most
dishes light. The interior, care
of India Mahdavi alumnus
Charlotte Biltgen, incorporates
recycled freight-train planks,
wabi-sabi Japanese tiles
and warm brass lighting,
reflecting the sincerity and
joy of the food writ large.

7

ROSA BONHEUR SUR SEINE

Quai d'Orsay, Port des Invalides
01 47 53 66 92
rosabonheur.fr
Open Mon–Sat 12pm–2am,
Sun 12pm–12am (summer;
see website for other times of
the year)
Metro: Invalides, Champs-
Élysées–Clemenceau

The Rosa Bonheur crew opened their first establishment up in the 19e's Parc des Buttes Chaumont (*see* p. 214) and have now brought the bonhomie to central Paris. They infuse all they do with a wild Provençal joie de vivre, and this jolly floating enterprise is no exception. Come aboard the overgrown houseboat moored by Pont Alexandre III for a long night of music and dancing beneath colourful lanterns and the odd plastic flamingo, or just drop by for a quiet afternoon drink-with-a-view on a terrace beanbag. Snacks are far from shabby: hot dogs, proper pizza, good-quality charcuterie, sardines, and dips of taramasalata, artichoke and soft goat's cheese. Pastis by the glass and bottles of rosé are the cheapest you'll find this side of a DIY Seine-side picnic.

8.

COUTUME
47 rue de Babylone
01 45 51 50 47
coutumecafe.com
Open Mon–Sat 8am–7pm,
Sun 10am–6pm
Metro: Vaneau, Saint-François-
Xavier

Parisian coffee pioneers Antoine Netien and his Australian partner Tom Clarke opened this café and one of the city's best-known roasteries in 2011 and now supply their beans to countless venues in France and Japan. The café is a mix of original shop mouldings, columns, woodwork, raw plasterwork, and industrial, lab-like elements that honour the production side of the business as well as make for an intriguing space. Parisians have been known to cross the river for Antoine and Tom's heaped weekend brunch dishes – with quinoa salads, poached eggs and fresh juices served alongside pastries, fry-ups, organic wine and craft beer, it's your choice whether to make it a day of detox or retox.

PARIS TIP
Stretching between the
Musée d'Orsay and the
Pont de l'Alma Les Berges
is a 2.3 kilometre strip
of green along the Seine
that's great for running,
strolling or riding while
taking in views of the Eiffel
Tower, the Louvre and the
Grand Palais.

TO
MAP RIGHT
(VIA AVENUE DES
← CHAMPS-ÉLYSÉES)

**LIBRAIRIE
ARTCURIAL
& CAFÉ** Franklin
D.Roosevelt

RUE DU CIRQUE

AVENUE GABRIEL

Jardin des
Champs-Élysées

Théâtre
Marigny

AVENUE DES CHAMPS-ÉLYSÉES

**MONTAIGNE
MARKET**

Théâtre du
Rond-Point

Square
de Berlin

AVENUE FRANKLIN-DELANO ROOSEVELT

IMPASSE D'ANTIN

**Champs-Élysées-
Clemenceau**

RUE JEAN
GOUJON

AVENUE DU
GÉNÉRAL EISENHOWER

AVENUE WINSTON-CHURCHILL

**LA TABLE
DU HUIT**

**Grand
Palais**

Palais de la
Découverte

**Petit
Palais**

RUE BAYARD

RUE FRANÇOIS 1ER

**MINI
PALAIS**

Musée des
Beaux-Arts
de la Ville
de Paris

COURS LA REINE

VOIE GEORGES POMPIDOU

COURS ALBERT 1ER

COURS LA REINE

PONT DES
INVALIDES

La   Seine

PONT
ALEXANDRE III

Framed by Napoleon's Arc de Triomphe, the tree-lined avenue of the Champs-Élysées is the well-known locale for La Fête Nationale (Bastille Day) parades and Tour de France finishes.

Beyond the neighbourhood's famed luxury shopping, politician-spotting and soaking in the rarefied atmosphere of grand residential streets, there's an impressive concentration of cultural riches spread across both arrondissements. These include the Palais de Tokyo, Musée d'Art Moderne, and the Grand and Petit palais art museums. The 16e – its straightforward nickname 'le seizième' a byword for wealth, prestige and power – is also home to Roland Garros Stadium, site of spring's fashion festival, er sorry, the French Open.

24   JUN 6016

SHOP
1 MONTAIGNE MARKET

SHOP, EAT AND DRINK
2 PUBLICIS DRUGSTORE
3 LIBRAIRIE ARTCURIAL & CAFÉ

17

EAT AND DRINK
4 VICTORIA 1836
5 LE CINQ
6 MONSIEUR BLEU
7 MINI PALAIS
8 LA TABLE DU HUIT

8E AND 16E:
CHAMPS-ÉLYSÉES
AND 'LE 16E'

VICTORIA
1836

PLACE
CHARLES
DE GAULLE

Charles
de Gaulle–
Étoile

Arc de
Triomphe
de l'Étoile

AVENUE DE FRIEDLAND

RUE RUDE

AVENUE FOCH

AVENUE VICTOR HUGO

RUE LORD BYRON

BALZAC

Hôtel
Balzac

8e

AVENUE DES CHAMPS-ÉLYSÉES

Le Lido

PUBLICIS
DRUGSTORE

George V

RUE

Hôtel
Amarante
Champs-
Élysées

VERNET

**TO
LIBRAIRIE
ARTCURIAL & CAFÉ,
MONTAIGNE MARKET,
LA TABLE DU HUIT
& MINI PALAIS
(SEE MAP LEFT)**

Kléber

RUE LAURISTON

RUE DU DÔME

KLÉBER

RUE DE LA PÉROUSE

AVENUE D'IÉNA

RUE NEWTON

RUE AUGUSTE VACQUERIE

RUE GALILÉE

Hôtel
Raphael

RUE JEAN GIRAUDOUX

RUE CHRISTOPHE COLOMB

The
Peninsula
Paris

RUE LA PÉROUSE

RUE DUMONT D'URVILLE

RUE KEPLER

MARCEAU

AVENUE

CHAILLOT

RUE JEAN GIRAUDOUX

RUE QUENTIN BAUCHART

AVENUE

Prince
de Galles

LE CINQ

RUE DE BELLOY

PLACE DES ÉTATS-UNIS

AVENUE D'IÉNA

RUE DE BASSANO

Hôtel
Élysées
Régencia

Hôtel
Élysées
Union

RUE GALILÉE

Square
Thomas
Jefferson

0   100 m

AVENUE PIERRE 1er DE SERBIE

IMPASSE DU DOCTEUR
JACQUES BERTILLON

AVENUE GEORGE V

RUE DE L'AMIRAL D'ESTAING

Galerie-
Musée
Baccarat

16e

RUE
GEORGES BIZET

RUE GEORGES BIZET

MARCEAU

RUE DE L'AMIRAL HAMELIN

RUE DE LÜBECK

AVENUE D'IÉNA

RUE FREYCINET

RUE DE SERBIE

RUE GOETHE

AVENUE

RUE

BOISSIÈRE

Musée National
des Arts
Asiatiques-
Guimet

AVENUE PIERRE 1er

RUE FREYCINET

RUE DE GALLIERA

RUE LÉONCE
REYNAUD

MARCEAU

RUE DE LONGCHAMP

Iéna

Palais Galliera–
Musée de la Mode
de la Ville
de Paris

Square
Brignolle-
Galliera

RUE DES
FRÈRES PÉRIER

Alma-
Marceau

AVENUE DU
PRÉSIDENT WILSON

AVENUE DU PRÉSIDENT WILSON

Palais
de Tokyo

Musée d'Art
Moderne

RUE GASTON
DE SAINT-PAUL

RUE DEBROUSSE

Shangri-La
Hotel

AVENUE D'IÉNA

RUE FRESNEL

RUE DE LA
MANUTENTION

MONSIEUR
BLEU

AVENUE DE NEW YORK

La Seine

1.

MONTAIGNE MARKET

57 avenue Montaigne, 8e
01 42 56 58 58
montaignemarket.com
Open Mon–Sat 10.30am–7pm
Metro: Champs-Élysées–
Clemenceau, Franklin D.
Roosevelt

Despite having clients that
include one-name models
(Kendall, Gigi) and conjoined-
name celebs (KimYe, aka Kim
Kardashian and Kanye West),
there's no need to fear the
shop assistant snarl at Liliane
Jossua's multibrand fashion
shop: it has some of the most
welcoming staff in luxuryland.
Two floors house over 100
clothing, accessory and
jewellery labels, making for a
heady shopping (or fantasy
shopping) experience indeed.
That's some breadth, but
there's also a good amount
of curatorial nous on display
(note Jossua's penchant for
black, more black and white).
Coo over the Azzedine Alaïa
leather and Lanvin lace,
and don't miss trying on the
Leetha cashmere pieces and
Reiss tees.

2.

PUBLICIS DRUGSTORE

133 avenue des Champs-
Élysées, 8e
01 44 43 75 07
publicisdrugstore.com
Open Mon–Fri 9am–2am,
Sat–Sun 10am–2am
Metro: Charles de
Gaulle–Étoile, George V

There's more than a little bit
of New York in this Champs-
Élysées ad-agency-owned
superstore. There's the name,
of course, and its range of
desire-inducing things is
American in scale. Then
there's the almost-always-
open ethos, a godsend for
the jetlagged wanderer
or the guilt-driven last-
minute present buyer. Pick
up everything you've been
meaning to buy but haven't
yet got around to (thanks
to those lunchtime rosés
by the Canal Saint-Martin):
eminently packable canisters
of Kusmi or Mariage Frères
tea, Pierre Hermé macarons,
Dinh Van jewellery, Martin
Margiela candles and Henri
Cartier-Bresson gift cards.
For other out-of-hours travel
emergencies, there's a
Champagne shop, a caviar
section, a pharmacy *and* a
basement l'Atelier de Joël
Robuchon (*see* p. 096).

1.

1.

1.

1.

2.

1.

3.

LIBRAIRIE ARTCURIAL & CAFÉ

7 rond-point des Champs-
Élysées, 8e
01 42 99 20 20
artcurial.com
Open Mon–Fri 9am–7pm,
Sat 10.30am–7pm (bookshop);
Mon–Sat 10am–11pm (café)
Metro: Franklin D. Roosevelt

Housed in a stunning 1844 hôtel particulier (grand townhouse), Artcurial is France's largest French-owned auction house. Down the hall from the museum-worthy auction exhibitions are two treats. The house's bookshop has an astounding range of art books and journals, covering the ancient world to the latest in the contemporary art and design scene. It also has a very well-curated selection of rare titles, limited-edition artists' books, prints and objects (the Sophie Calle plate goes in the hand luggage, right?). Across the way, Italian design reigns at the conservatory café, where you can pore over your purchases with a glass of Piedmont's finest and a plate of carpaccio or burrata cheese.

VICTORIA 1836

12 rue de Presbourg, 16e
01 44 17 97 72
victoria-1836.com
Open Mon–Fri 8am–11.30pm,
Sat 11am–11.30pm
Metro: Charles de Gaulle–Étoile

- -

The last stone of the Arc de Triomphe was laid in 1836, 30 years after Napoleon proclaimed to his men 'You will return home through arches of triumph!'. Named for this imperial moment, Victoria 1836 is itself a triumphal return, its stunning interior fashioned from the burnt-out shell of the famous l'Arc restaurant. Designer Sarah Lavoine makes use of original stonework and a particularly elegant palette of black, white and blue. Dishes like crab ravioli with lemongrass emulsion and foie gras with Sarawak pepper are as on-trend as the decor, and an extensive Champagne list sets the tone from the get-go. As this is a project of Benjamin Patou, a well-known tête bien fête (i.e. one of the city's biggest event organisers), expect top-notch people-watching: hello, Mick Jagger!

5.

LE CINQ

31 avenue George V, 8e
01 49 52 71 54
restaurant-lecinq.com
Open Mon–Sun 7–10am,
12.30–2.30pm & 7–10pm
Metro: Alma-Marceau, George V

The Four Season's traditional grey and gold dining room has beautiful views of the hotel's courtyard and the trimmings and theatrical formality you'd expect at such a legendary place. Chef Christian Le Squer's dishes draw on classic French culinary techniques while often being highly inventive; if there's a constant, it's his precise and unifying way with flavour and texture. Per-course prices are, as is the way with these three-star dining rooms, staggering, but the four-course lunch menu comes in at not much more than a single course à la carte, and usually offers choices of both starters and mains. It's also a lovely spot for breakfast, with a wonderfully authentic Japanese option.

6.

MONSIEUR BLEU

20 avenue de New York, 16e
01 47 20 90 47
monsieurbleu.com
Open Mon–Sun 12pm–2am
Metro: Iéna, Alma-Marceau

There's an extraordinary view of the Eiffel Tower from the fair-weather terrace at Monsier Bleu, part of Palais de Tokyo, the city's largest and, at times, most provocative contemporary art museum. If it's too cold out, rest assured that the restaurant's inside view is not so shabby either. The building dates back to 1937, and, although the fit-out by architect Joseph Dirand is as recent as 2012, there's still a dark between-the-wars glamour at work. Nine-metre-high ceilings, expanses of brass, original Lalique crystal panels and black marble provide the 'wow' factor, while generously spaced tables and Eero Saarinen chairs upholstered in hues of pale moss keep things contemporary and human-scaled. Food is a mix of Gallic comfort (calf's liver, roast chicken) and international hit-parade items (lobster roll, fish carpaccio), but can't help but play second fiddle to the fabulous decor.

PARIS TIP
Parc Monceau makes for an idyllic, and suitably elegant, escape with its English-style follies and rambling trails. Look out for the Egyptian pyramid, the windmill and the Renaissance-era arcade of the original Hôtel de Ville.

7.

MINI PALAIS

3 avenue Winston Churchill, 16e
01 42 56 42 42
minipalais.com
Open Mon–Sun 10am–2am
Metro: Champs-Élysées–
Clemenceau, Invalides

This not-so-mini restaurant
occupies a prime, pretty
corner of the Beaux-Arts
beauty that is the Grand
Palais, the city's blockbuster
exhibition space and
museum. There's a wonderful
sense of occasion to the
dining room, with dark-wood
furniture, oak floors, exposed
iron beams, and dramatically
back-lit busts and sculptures.
Although its all-day hours and
pleasant-but-not-polished
service make it far from a
fine-dining option, there's
much-better-than-average
bistro food on offer, with steak
tartare and the like, but also
Asian-inflected dishes such
as cod glazed in tamarind.
If it's warm, opt for a terrace
table under the magnificent
columns of the neoclassical
peristyle, with views to the
Pont d'Alexandre III.

8.

LA TABLE DU HUIT

8 rue Jean Goujon, 8e
01 40 74 64 95
latableduhuit.fr
Open Mon–Sun 7am–1.30am
(breakfast 7–10am, lunch
12–2.30pm, tapas 6–7pm,
dinner 7–10.30pm, Sunday
brunch 11am–3pm)
Metro: Champs-Élysées–
Clemenceau, Franklin D.
Roosevelt

Dreamlike vignettes fill the
hotel La Maison Champs-
Élysées – care of fashion
house Maison Martin
Margiela – and its restaurant,
La Table du Huit (aka 'le 8') is
no exception. Draped in slip
cloths, classical Louis chairs
become ghostly things, while
expanses of surreal black-
and-white trompe l'oeils
face off against a green,
glowing internal garden. If
you're eating outside, the
chandeliered world gives
way to what feels like the
bowels of a spaceship, a
shiny metallic corridor that
transports you into a beautiful
(if surprisingly conventional)
garden. Dining is aimed
at well-heeled shoppers
(carefully executed, non-
confrontational) and Sunday
brunches are lavish, offering
the additional temptation of a
'Champagne at will' option.

and 16e: Champs-Élysées and 'le 16e'

The ninth is an arrondissement of wildly diverse personalities. Place Pigalle still has its tour buses and sleaze, but the hostess bars of rue Frochot are fast disappearing, replaced by venues serving artisan cocktails. The neighbourhood's rapid hipsterfication demanded a snappy rebranding, and thus we have SoPi (south of Pigalle).

The slightly more mature Martyrs neighbourhood is centred around the gastronomically inclined rue des Martyrs. Several blocks below are the Grands Boulevards with their iconic department stores Galeries Lafayette and Printemps, along with the opulent, utterly breathtaking Palais Garnier, home to the Paris Opéra, for which the surrounding neighbourhood is named.

9E: OPÉRA, PIGALLE, SOPI AND MARTYRS

24 JUN 8076

SHOP, EAT AND DRINK
1 Sept Cinq

EAT
2 Mesdemoiselles Madeleines
3 Rose Bakery
4 Un Thé Dans le Jardin

EAT AND DRINK
5 Le Richer
6 Artisan
7 La Maison Mère
8 Petrelle
9 Grand Pigalle Hotel Bar
10 Buvette Gastrothèque

La Boule Noire
Square d'Anvers
RUE DE ROCHECHOUART
RUE DE DUNKERQUE
BOULEVARD DE ROCHECHOUART
RUE DES MARTYRS
RUE VIOLLET-LE-DUC
RUE LALLIER
RUE CRETET
RUE BOCHART DE SARON
RUE JEAN-BAPTISTE SAY
AVENUE
AVENUE TRUDAINE
TRUDAINE
RUE DE ROCHECHOUART

PIGALLE

BARBÈS

Hôtel Caravelle

ARTISAN

⊠ **PETRELLE** ●

RUE PETRELLE

CITÉ MALESHERBES

◈ **KB CAFESHOP**

RUE BOCHART DE SARON

RODIER

RUE TURGOT

RUE THIMONNIER

RUE LENTONNET

LA MAISON MÈRE

RUE

CONDORCET

RUE CONDORCET

RUE DE LA TOUR D'AUVERGNE

CITÉ CONDORCET

RUE CONDORCET

● **ROSE BAKERY**

MESDEMOISELLES MADELEINES

CITÉ FÉNELON

Hôtel La Tour d'Auvergne

RUE DE LA TOUR D'AUVERGNE

RUE DE ROCHECHOUART

RUE DE MAUBEUGE

SQUARE DE MAUBEUGE

Résidence du Pré

RUE DE CHANTILLY

RUE PIERRE SEMARD

RUE DES MARTYRS

RUE MANUEL

RUE MILTON

RUE DE L'AGENT BAILLY

RUE DE

RODIER

9e

RUE DE BELLEFOND

TO UN THÉ DANS LE JARDIN, GRAND PIGALLE HOTEL BAR, BATON ROUGE, BUVETTE GASTROTHÈQUE, SEPT CINQ & GLASS (SEE MAP LEFT)

RUE DES

RUE CHORON

RUE HIPPOLYTE LEBAS

RUE DE MAUBEUGE

RUE DE ROCHECHOUART

RUE ROCHAMBEAU

■ Hôtel du Pré

Hôtel Williams Opera

MAYRAN

Square de Montholon

RUE LAMARTINE

RUE MONTHOLON

RUE DE MONTHOLON

RUE DE PAPILLON

RUE BUFFAULT

RUE CADET

RUE LA FAYETTE

RUE RIBOUTTÉ

⊠

RUE DE CHÂTEAUDUN

🚊 **Cadet**

RUE BLEUE

DRINK

11 BATON ROUGE

12 GLASS

RUE LA FAYETTE

PASSAGE DES DEUX SŒURS

SAULNIER

RUE DE TRÉVISE

△ N

RUE DE TRÉVISE

RUE AMBROISE THOMAS

RUE DU FAUBOURG POISSONNIÈRE

🚊 **Le Peletier**

RUE DU FAUBOURG

Musée de la Franc-Maçonnerie

LesFeux de la Rampe

Folies Bergère

RUE RICHER

RUE RICHER

CITÉ

LE RICHER ●

RUE DE PROVENCE

RUE CHAUCHAT

RUE DROUOT

RUE DE LA GRANGE BATELIÈRE

MONTMARTRE

RUE GEOFFROY MARIE

RUE DE LA BOULE ROUGE

RUE DE TRÉVISE

Théâtre Trévise

RUE DU CONSERVATOIRE

Villa Opéra Drouot

RUE DE MONTYON

RUE SAINTE-CÉCILE

RUE ROSSINI

0   100 m

JUN 80T6

1.

SEPT CINQ
54 rue Notre-Dame de Lorette
09 83 55 05 95
sept-cinq.com
Open Tues–Sat 11am–8pm,
Sun 2–6pm
Metro: Saint-Georges, Pigalle

The seven (sept) and cinq (five) of this shop's name references the '75' prefix of the Parisian postcode: yes, everything here is made in Paris. Two young business-school grads, Lorna Moquet and Audrey Gallier, have brought together Mimilamour's witty jewellery, beautiful leather bags from MeilleurAmi, loafers, boots and ballet flats from Bobbies, and many more genuinely local products. Look out for the 'Weekend à Paris' candle from Ines de la Fressange – raspberry, peach, frescia and leather notes are designed to conjure the scent of a Parisian's elegant handbag. The little salon-style café on site even serves locally brewed beer.

MESDEMOISELLES MADELEINES

37 rue des Martyrs
01 53 16 28 82
mllesmadeleines.com
Open Tues–Sat 10am–7.30pm,
Sun 10am–2pm &
3.30–6.30pm
Metro: Saint-Georges, Pigalle

After waves of pastry 'mono-produits' – shops selling just one patisserie staple (first the macaron, then the éclair and the choux-puff) – this Martyrs newcomer could mean the reign of the madeleine is nigh. These little shell-shaped butter cakes are traditionally, and intentionally, plain (all the better to dip in a fragrant tisane, as Proust mused), but star pastry chef Stéphane Bour has reimagined them for a new century. Using butter from Normandy and the best French flour, they bear roll-off-the-tongue French girls' names – Garence, Clemence and Apolline – and are variously flavoured and filled with citrus, hazelnuts, ganache, caramel and even savoury herbs.

3.

ROSE BAKERY
46 rue des Martyrs
01 42 82 12 80
Open Mon–Sun 9am–6pm
Metro: Saint-Georges, Pigalle

English expat Rose Carrarini
and her French husband
Jean-Charles opened this
Anglo-French tearoom in
2002. Its rapid and runaway
success – there's been two
Rose Bakery cookbooks
and there are now offshoot
cafés in the Marais, New
York, London, Tokyo and
Seoul – created something
of a trend in big healthy
salads and heaped vegetable
quiches. Carrarini has also
turned Parisians onto earthy,
homey Anglo baking: carrot
cake, brownies and citrus-
scented pound loaves have
become staples on her
menus. This original café,
with its expressionist murals,
schoolroom chairs and
overflowing displays, remains
the warm and happily
chaotic place it always has
been (and, charmingly, you
might spot Rose herself –
she lives nearby and can
often still be found in the
tearoom's kitchen).

4.

UN THÉ DANS LE JARDIN
Musée de la Vie Romantique,
16 rue Chaptal
01 55 31 95 67
cafe-vie-romantique.com
Open Tues–Sun 10am–6pm
(mid-Mar–mid-Oct)
Metro: Saint-Georges, Blanche

Down a cobblestone alley in
the Nouvelle Athènes district,
this salon de thé (tearoom) is
set within the walled, rose-
and fuchsia-filled garden
of a stunning freestanding
1830s villa. Once the home
of painter Ary Scheffer,
fellow painters Delacroix
and Ingres and musicians
Liszt, Rossini and Chopin
were often invited round for
Friday night drinks. Today it
houses the Musée de la Vie
Romantique, dedicated to the
writer George Sand, Chopin's
lover, with portraits and
personal objects displayed
on the ground floor. Despite
the slight catering, the green
tearoom and its garden tables
are a rare Parisian delight:
human-scaled, hidden,
fragrant and full of birdsong,
a perfect place for a pot of tea
and some romantic reverie.

3.

PARIS TIP
Splendid early–19th century Nouvelle Athènes (New Athens) townhouses can still be seen on and near rue de la Tour-des-Dames (*see map* p. 114). Neoclassical beauties include the wonderful Musée Gustave Moreau, the painter's former home and light-filled studio on rue de la Rochefoucauld.

4.

3.

4.

4.

LE RICHER

2 rue Richer
lericher.com
Open Mon–Sun 8am–11pm
Metro: Poissonnière, Bonne
Nouvelle

A corner café that's been
stripped back to bare, though
rather fetching, bones, Le
Richer offers one of Paris'
most stress-free dining
options. Show up at 7pm and
you're all but guaranteed
a table; after that singles
and couples can usually
nab a seat at the bar to dine
throughout the night. The
space's thoughtful simplicity
extends to the daily lunch
and dinner menus: novel
combinations and global
influences are there, but
fabulous seasonal produce is
always the star – guinea fowl
is paired with mint, walnuts
and Corsican sheep's cheese,
while duck comes smoked
and braised with romaine
lettuce. Different wines by
the glass appear each service,
giving the young, handsome
sommeliers a chance to be
delightfully opinionated and
uncannily intuitive about
what you'll really, really like.

ARTISAN

14 rue Bochart de Saron
01 48 74 65 38
artisan-bar.fr
Open Tues–Sat 7pm–2am
Metro: Anvers, Pigalle

There's nothing dark or
mysterious, gimmicky
or glam about this big-
windowed bar. Instead
there's a beautiful zinc
counter, extremely well-
crafted cocktails and a crew
of laid-back locals. The drinks
list changes according to
the availability of fruit and
vegetables, along with the
mood of the bartender; wines
take a back seat but are still
well sourced. While those
tipples might be the raison
d'être for your visit, you'll
be very pleasantly surprised
by what comes out of the
kitchen, which dishes up
some of the neighbourhood's
most interesting eating
(and, another bonus, food is
served until midnight). Little
dishes, often plays on French
classics (say, a tartare or
roast lamb), are stylishly and
prettily presented, but are
also full of substantial flavour
and interest.

7.

LA MAISON MÈRE

4 rue de Navarin
01 42 81 11 00
Open Mon–Sat 12–3pm &
7pm–2am, Sun 12–4pm &
7pm–2am
Metro: Pigalle, Saint-Georges

The aptly named Maison Mère – 'mother's house' – may look the picture of a neo-bistro, with a beautiful industrial fit-out scattered with vintage pieces. But no, instead you'll find pure comfort fodder: burgers, other diner-style favourites like crab cakes, a few home-style French dishes such as roast chicken, and some cute menu idiosyncrasies like a parmesan-crisp-enclosed veal burger. The chilled staff are some of the friendliest in the city, greeting everyone like regulars, and the terrace is a sunny and convivial spot. If you're suffering from a mammoth SoPi hangover (it happens), this is a good spot for Sunday brunch.

PETRELLE

34 rue Petrelle
01 42 82 11 02
petrelle.fr
Open Tues–Sat 8–10pm
Metro: Anvers

Pop into Petrelle early to make a booking and you'll probably find owner-chef-decorator Jean-Luc André and his sole waiter chowing down on a meal as the aroma of a slow braise wafts from the kitchen and the house cat looks on. Petrelle is a timeless and particularly Parisian proposition. There's the layer-upon-layer beautiful eccentricity of the dining room itself ('impossibly romantic' in this case is more truth than cliché). Then there's André's cooking: lovingly prepared meat and fish dishes from trusted suppliers paired with his home-grown vegetables and traditional sauces. And those meringues adorning the entry table? They'll be proffered as a take-home treat as you contentedly bid your host 'Bonsoir'.

9.

GRAND PIGALLE HOTEL BAR
29 rue Victor Massé
01 85 73 12 02
grandpigalle.com
Open Mon–Sun 7am–2am
Metro: Pigalle, Saint-Georges

With windows opening onto SoPi's most vibrant corner (not to mention the gates of what was once the sprawling estate of Toulouse-Lautrec), this rez-de-chaussée (ground floor) place feels more like 'the local' than the bar of a grand hotel. GPH is, in fact, quite an intimate affair, with few everyday hotel details to detract from its moody atmospherics. Pull up a blue-velvet stool or grab a window table for wine, cocktails and sardines or charcuterie. The point of difference here is what might be the city's largest selection of Italian wines by the glass or bottle, not to mention the attentive, smiling sommeliers who are passionate advocates of their product.

10.

BUVETTE GASTROTHÈQUE
28 rue Henry Monnier
01 44 63 41 71
buvette.com
Open Mon–Sun 8.30am–12am
Metro: Saint-Georges, Pigalle

Buvette, a traditional Parisian bistro, began life in Greenwich Village in 2011, so there's something rather discombobulating about Jody Williams' Paris 'transplant'. But any globalisation jitters will soon fade once you take note of the well-sourced regional French wine list. Traditionally buvettes are casual stalls where there are no set meal times (sounds suspiciously like New World snacking, no?), and it's this spirit that informs Buvette Gastrothèque, which otherwise presents as Parisian as can be. The menu is mostly traditional with a twist, like brandade de morue (salt cod puree) or hachis parmentier (French shepherd's pie), along with inventive sandwiches; all are small and can be shared. Weekend brunches are hearty and popular, and puddings – mousse, tarte tatin, moelleux au chocolate (chocolate fondant cake) – sublimely old school.

11.

BATON ROUGE
62 rue Notre-Dame de Lorette
06 52 90 36 42
batonrouge.paris
Open Mon–Sat 6pm–2am
Metro: Saint-Georges, Pigalle

There's a time for dancing
to electro-pop and drinking
vodka from a plastic cup at
the hostess-turned-hipster-
bars of rue Jean-Baptiste
Pigalle, and that usually
comes sometime way after
midnight. Before that, head
to this nearby New Orleans
meets *Elle Decor* cocktail
den. Most of the drinks list is
inspired by the 1930s tome
*Famous New Orleans Drinks
and How to Mix 'Em*, so get
into the bayou spirit with a
Creole concoction of bourbon,
Cajun spice, egg yolk and
milk, or the killer house
drink that mixes cognac,
absinthe and Champagne.
Perhaps because the soul of
Louisiana is forever French,
the Americana immersion
here feels rich rather
than derivative.

12.

GLASS
7 rue Frochot
09 80 72 98 83
glassparis.com
Open Mon–Sun 7pm–2am
Metro: Saint-Georges, Pigalle

In the frantic nocturnal
world that is rue Frochot,
Glass is a 2012 pioneer. This
bar–nightclub is still one
of the Old Vice Row's best,
with a carefully cultivated
down-and-dirty vibe. Decor
becomes irrelevant in the
darkness: the focus is on
the bar, the DJ booth and
on designer Adrian Rubi-
Dentzel's mesmerising,
pulsing dance floor. Brooklyn
IPA is on tap and beer of
all sorts finds its way into
surprising areas of the
drinks list (the Kiki Smith
cocktail is a gin, lemon,
shiso leaves and Belgian
lambic beer inhibition killer
of epic proportions). Got the
Monday night blues? Join
the city's hospitality crews
who party till way past official
closing time.

Clotilde is the author of the long-running blog *Chocolate & Zucchini* and has published four books, including *Clotilde's Edible Adventures in Paris* and *The French Market Cookbook*. Her stories and recipes have appeared in publications in the US, France and the UK, including *The New York Times Magazine* and *Elle à Table*.

What are the best food finds in the 9e?

The rue des Martyrs area (*see map* p. 115) is heaven for food lovers. There are the different shops lining the street itself (don't miss the waffles from Comptoir Belge, chocolates from Henri Le Roux, Beillevaire's cheese, pastries from Sébastien Gaudard, boutique olive oils at Première Pression Provence, Les Papilles Gourmandes' fabulous charcuterie and wonderful roast chicken from Plume), but also the Anvers green market on Friday afternoons, and all the gems tucked away on adjoining streets.

What's your favourite iconic Paris moment?

Despite having lived in Paris most of my life, I never tire of admiring the Eiffel Tower, and I am like a child when it starts twinkling on

the hour at night. I also have fond memories of having lunch up there, at the Jules Verne restaurant on the second floor, with an incredible view.

Where do you go for coffee?

KB CaféShop in southern Pigalle (*see map* p. 115) is a favourite haunt of mine, with a lovely terrace beneath the trees and very good coffee. I like to catch up with friends or have professional meetings there.

Where do you go to escape?

When the weather is nice, it's quite lovely to have brunch at the Hôtel Particulier in Montmartre, a hidden hotel with small tables in a lush and super charming garden.

Home to the grand twin train stations Gare du Nord and Gare de L'Est, the 10e has, over the last decade, become one of Paris' new hot spots. At its heart is the pretty, party-hard Canal Saint-Martin, a still-working waterway that links the Seine with Paris' north-east.

Between here and the broad, pedestrianised Place de la République there's a spot-on collection of Parisian fashion favourites, making for one of Paris' least harried shopping destinations. Heading east there's a gentrification face-off in Faubourg Saint-Denis. The once shabby, if eternally effervescent micro-quartier, known for its grocers and African hair salons, is rapidly morphing into one of the city's most fashionable bar and restaurant strips.

24   JUN 8016

SHOP
1 Broc'Martel
2 Artazart

SHOP AND EAT
3 La Trésorerie

EAT
4 Du Pain et Des Idées
5 Liberté

17

6 Ten Belles
7 Holybelly
8 Le Verre Volé sur Mer

EAT AND DRINK
9 Faubourg Saint-Denis 52
10 Vivant Table
11 La Cave à Michel

10E: CANAL SAINT-MARTIN, RÉPUBLIQUE AND FAUBOURG SAINT-DENIS

1.

BROC'MARTEL

12 rue Martel
01 48 24 53 43
brocmartel.com
Open Mon–Sat 1.30–7pm
Metro: Château d'Eau

Laurence Peyrelade's delicious vintage and industrial shop sits slap-bang in the middle of rue Martel, a café-filled but defiantly local strip. Her selection of 'curiosities' – fairground fittings and ephemera, shop signage, industrial lighting – indeed seems ready-made for those who reside in the high-ceilinged lofts of the city's north-east. But never fear: she also has an intriguing collection of smaller pieces (beautiful rattan mirrors, hat moulds, ceramics). If you're prepared to ship your finds home, her other speciality is chairs, including the metalwork of Tolix, Multipls and Fibrocit and the 1950s beauties by Tapiovaara, Baumann and Knoll.

2.

ARTAZART

83 Quai de Valmy
01 40 40 24 00
artazart.com
Open Mon–Fri 10.30am–7.30pm, Sat 11am–7.30pm, Sun 2–8pm
Metro: République, Jacques Bonsergent

This canal-side bookshop and gallery ups the ante with its vibrant orange exterior and continues to push boundaries inside with its inspiring, sometimes challenging, collection of art and design books and magazines. It was Paris' first shop dedicated to the 'graphic image', opened in 2000 by Carl Huguenin, Jérôme Fournel and retail veteran, Serge Bensimon (of Bensimon Home Autour du Monde; *see* p. 036). Three overstuffed rooms make for a wonderful sense of discovery; alongside the printed matter there are Lomo cameras and Freitag bags for sale and a culinary area with beautiful cookware and cookbooks. The gallery has hosted names from across the spectrum of contemporary art and design, from photographers Martin Parr and Antoine D'Agata to designer Matali Crasset; book signings and rambunctious openings are a regular event.

1.

1.

2.

2.

2.

2.

3.

LA TRÉSORERIE

11 rue du Château d'Eau
01 40 40 20 46
latresorerie.fr
Open Wed–Sat 11.30am–7pm
Metro: République

Once home to the district's treasury (hence the name 'trésorerie'), this high-ceilinged, bar-windowed warehouse is today packed with a delightfully domestic kind of bounty. Three friends, Elsa Coustals, Lino Landau and Denis Geffrault went into business with the aim of selling utilitarian things that are: a) made in Europe by small manufacturers (over a third are in fact made in France); b) made to last; and c) produced as sustainably as possible. These philosophical underpinnings are noble but also deliver: La Trésorerie's homewares, from linen dish cloths and l'Econome steak knives to Gien porcelain dinner sets and lamb's-wool blankets, have rich histories, tactility and true quotidian beauty. At the front, airy **Café Smörgås** serves up excellent coffee and Swedish treats.

DU PAIN ET DES IDÉES

34 rue Yves Toudic
01 42 40 44 52
dupainetdesidees.com
Open Mon–Fri 6.45am–8pm
Metro: Jacques Bonsergent

This neighbourhood boulangerie (bakery) looks the part – all gleaming 19th-century shop fittings – and turns out what many Parisians, including Michelin-starred chef Alain Ducasse, consider to be the city's best bread. Yes, there is often a queue out the door, but it's marked by a comradely sense of anticipation. Once you're inside, staff are charming and star boulanger Christophe Vasseur's pain des amis is your reward. This loaf, with its charred, flavour-filled crusts, makes amends for every wan baguette you've ever encountered. What else will need trying? Pastry swirls studded with pistachios, a pain brioché scented with saffron and honey, and a crisp-shelled tart with a fruit for every season (perhaps plum, pear, cherry or peach).

5.

LIBERTÉ

39 rue des Vinaigriers
01 42 05 51 76
libertepatisserieboulangerie.com
Open Mon–Fri 7.30am–8pm,
Sat 6.30am–7.30pm
Metro: Jacques Bonsergent

Interiors fans will love the stylish, modern, industrial mashup at this boulangerie-patisserie, with its monumental marble counter and strikingly distressed ceiling tile work and rusted columns. Watch the open kitchen from one of the tables by the window: Benoît Castel – once the head pâtissier at Bon Marché's La Grande Épicerie (*see* p. 094) – is known for his rustic, character-filled breads and delicate cakes and pastries. The financiers (the original French equivalent of the Anglo-Australian friand) are dense and fragrant, or try a 'bobo au rhum', a rum baba served in a Duralex coffee glass, the pastryman's sly quip at his neighbourhood's predominantly bobo demographic. In the 20e, there's another fabulously rustic Liberté at 150 rue de Ménilmontant.

TEN BELLES

10 rue de la Grange aux Belles
01 42 40 90 78
tenbelles.com
Open Mon–Fri 8am–6pm,
Sat–Sun 9am–7pm
Metro: Jacques Bonsergent

When Ten Belles opened back in 2010, good coffee was a rare thing indeed in Paris. This café's siren song of a perfectly made flat white helped transform picturesque little rue de la Grange aux Belles, one block back from the Canal Saint-Martin, into a bobo enclave, and Ten Belles is now flanked by a florist, an organic produce store and makers' ateliers. An international barista army serves up expertly made espresso and filter coffee with beans from co-owner Thomas Lehoux' Belleville Brûlerie roastery, along with a menu of Anglo-inflected café food care of Le Bal Café in the 18e (*see* p. 203): think brownies and granola but also scones, sausage rolls and over-stuffed sandwiches.

7.

HOLYBELLY

19 rue Lucien Sampaix
09 73 60 13 64
holybel.ly
Open Mon, Thurs & Fri 9am–
5pm, Sat–Sun 10am–5pm
Metro: Jacques Bonsergent

Subway-tiled Holybelly might be the poster child for the hipster annexation of north-east Paris – ironically the annexation that expat Brooklynite hipsters keep complaining about – but seriously, what's not to like about good coffee and big breakfasts? Parisians Nico Alary and Sarah Mouchot honed their barista and kitchen chops in Melbourne and Vancouver and deliver the most genuinely sunny welcome in the city, along with excellent coffee served in equally sunny signature yellow cups. Mornings start with pancakes or maybe eggs and smashed avocado. The lunch menu's focus is on fresh seasonal ingredients and big bold flavours, and might include French standards like ragout of beef cheek or New World upstarts like fish tacos, and kale, beet and quinoa salad.

LE VERRE VOLÉ SUR MER

53 rue de Lancry
01 48 03 21 38
leverrevole.fr
Open Mon–Sun 12–2pm
& 7–11pm
Metro: République, Jacques
Bonsergent, Gare de l'Est

Cyril Bordarier's Le Verre Volé is a Canal Saint-Martin legend, a tiny cave à manger – wine bar and shop – showcasing natural and small-producer wines with some seriously good cooking. This, his new baby, specialises in fish and seafood, as the 'by the sea' suffix suggests. A gleeful octopuses garden mural dominates the small shopfront space and, like the original Verre, the decor is more by default than by design. Lunch is done bento-box style: sushi, sashimi, miso-glazed salmon, lotus-root salads and the like. While there's still the occasional Japanese influence at dinnertime, the menu takes in both Atlantic- and Mediterranean-style seafood dishes, from butter-glazed scallops and broth-doused Breton whelks to raw plates and grilled red mullet with herb pesto. Staff will happily talk you through any sea creatures that prove unfamiliar, and also recommend smart choices from the short natural wine list.

9.

FAUBOURG SAINT-DENIS 52
52 rue du Faubourg Saint-Denis
Open Mon–Sun 8am–12am
(meals 12–2.30pm & 7–11pm)
Metro: Château d'Eau

Charles Compagnon, who gave us L'Office and then Le Richer (*see* p. 120), again works his magic at this restaurant-bar-café. Its concrete-walled and radically stripped-back space has a surprising warmth and intimacy and is somewhere locals drop in for a coffee, or a plate of cheese, great wines by the glass and a chat with the happy, handsome staff. Lunch and dinner may require more planning – no reservations are taken – but it's easy enough to snare a table if you arrive early or wait it out at the bar (hardly a chore, with those aforementioned happy, handsome staff buzzing about). The small menu offers four or so choices per course; expect pretty, flavour-filled and generally happy-making neo-bistro dishes.

PARIS TIP
Sign spotters and romantics should look out for the cluster of poetically named streets around rue du Faubourg Saint-Denis: rue de Fidelite, passage du Desire, rue de Paradis, and, maybe because these things often do end in tears, rue de Bleu.

VIVANT TABLE

43 rue des Petites Écuries
01 42 46 43 55
vivantparis.com
Open Mon–Fri 12–2pm (lunch),
Mon–Sat 7pm &
9.30pm (dinner sittings)
Metro: Bonne Nouvelle,
Château d'Eau

This tiny bare-tabled restaurant, filled with extraordinary Belle Époque tile work that vividly tells the story of its former life as an exotic apiary, is one of Paris' most romantic restaurants (note, if Champagne and chandeliers signal romance for you, we might not be on the same page here …). Small local suppliers are behind every dish, providing hormone-free meat, biodynamic vegetables and small-production natural wines. Dinner is a dimmed-lights multi-course affair, but the lunch menu is super value and still offers up two or three courses that reference French technique and sing with colour and deeply gratifying flavours. Next door, Vivant's contemporary marble-and-iron cave à manger – wine bar and shop – serves equally delightful small plates.

LA CAVE À MICHEL

36 rue Sainte-Marthe
01 42 45 94 47
Open Wed–Sun 3pm–12am
Metro: Belleville

Place Sainte-Marthe used to be somewhere you went to down a few pressions (tap beers) until Romain Tischenko, winner of the TV show *Top Chef* in 2010, and his brother Maxime opened upmarket restaurant Le Galopin. For those who prefer keeping their Sainte-Marthe nights casual, they've opened nearby wine bar La Cave à Michel, which is a winning combination of easy (no bookings), animated (often standing room only) and thoughtful about what comes out of its bar and tiny kitchen. Fabrice Mansouri, a veteran 'caviste', or cellar man, enthusiastically pours mostly natural, though never faddish, wines that are often made by friends. A meal can be put together from small sharing plates – say, flash-fried octopus, sweet green peppers with Basque ham, artichokes with pomelo and fromage frais – each a pared-back, precise taste of stellar ingredients.

CHEZ CASIMIR

6 rue de Belzunce
01 48 78 28 80
Open Mon–Fri 11.30am–3pm & 6.30–11pm, Sat–Sun 10am–6pm
Metro: Gare du Nord, Poissonnière

This bistro is tucked away behind the Saint-Vincent-de-Paul church, just ten minutes' stroll from the throng of Gare du Nord and sharing the sunny side of the street, and an owner, with upmarket **Chez Michel** and the endearingly eccentric **Pointe du Grouin** bar. Locals come here for generous, well-priced set menus of western and south-western French cooking. Dishes are far from fancy but use excellent produce: say a head-on certified Bresse-bred chicken, seasonal, perfectly cooked vegetables and organic wines. At meal's end you may already be well fed, but the thrill of the help-yourself cheese tray can't be underestimated. The traou mad ('good things' in Breton) brunch is possibly Paris' most bountiful, fun and ridiculously good value.

143

13.

LE COMPTOIR GÉNÉRAL

80 Quai de Jemmapes
01 44 88 24 48
lecomptoirgeneral.com
Open Mon–Sun 11am–2am
Metro: Jacques Bonsergent,
Goncourt

At this sprawling cool-kids' theme park of some 600 square metres, it's worth buying an apéro-hour rum-and-ginger just so you can wander through the brocante-jammed rooms and lush courtyard garden. This non-profit's mission statement says it all: 'whomever you may be, this hideaway, this temple of ghetto culture, shall be open to you every day of the week'. And hideaway it is: find it down a cobbled laneway, through an unmarked door. Come early for the Franco-African weekend brunch or stay late any night of the week for excellent world, reggae or Afro-funk DJs and an all-embracing, all-dancing, big-drinking crowd. There are also second-hand stalls, art exhibitions and coffee if you find yourself here during the day.

14.

LE SYNDICAT

51 rue du Faubourg Saint-Denis
Open Mon–Sat 6pm–2am
Metro: Château d'Eau

Look past the peeling posters to the gold lamé curtains within. This grunge-luxe, hip-hop-drenched drinking hole is a self-proclaimed 'Organisation de Défense des Spiritueux Français', created by Sullivan Doh and Romain Le Mouellic with the express aim to French-up the artisan cocktail. Cocktails here use Cognac and Armagnac – spirits most young French people associate with their grandparents – along with beautiful boutique French gins, absinthe, eau de vies (fruit brandies) and some surprise regional rarities. The creative list goes to town but the 'classiques' are equally charming, and include a made-in-France 'gen tonique' done with Pontarlier gentian liqueur and a herb-infused house-made tonic water.

14.

14.

13.

13.

13.

14.

Marie Macon and business partner Anne-Laure Lesquoy create collections of witty, exquisitely crafted, hand-embroidered brooches, patches and leather goods under the Macon & Lesquoy label. Marie has lived and worked in the centre of the 10e for over ten years.

How do you define contemporary Parisian style?

Paris is a mixture of creators who are not from Paris: a patchwork, a melting pot of internationalism always passed through a prism of French quality. It's a certain idea of luxury, the desire for work to be well done, which is a legacy of the high-end artisans and haute couture masters. To quote my partner Anne-Laure: 'the lining is as important as the jacket'.

Where do you go for coffee?

I go to Oberkampf to the old bar-tabacs – I hate places with a 'concept'! I like a place where you might bump into your old neighbours, because it is places like that that really contribute to the spirit of a city. I am a bit nostalgic for this Paris.

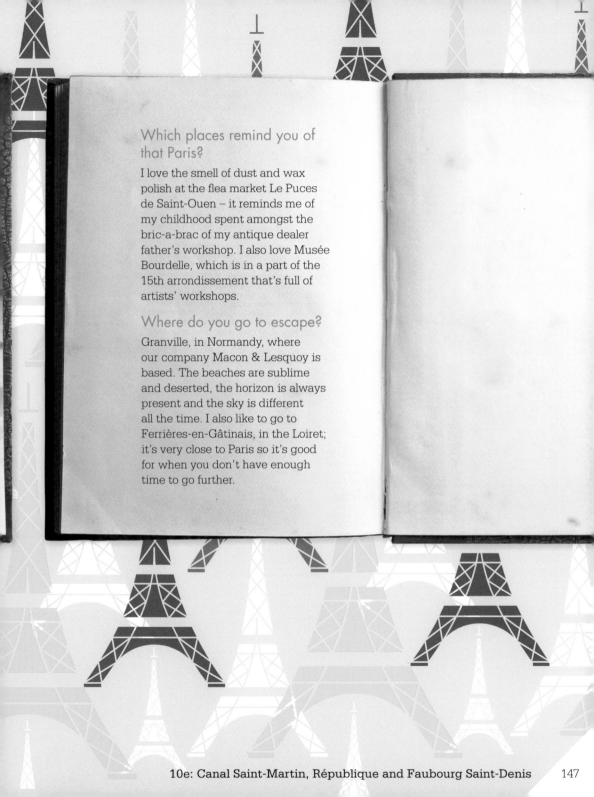

Which places remind you of that Paris?

I love the smell of dust and wax polish at the flea market Le Puces de Saint-Ouen – it reminds me of my childhood spent amongst the bric-a-brac of my antique dealer father's workshop. I also love Musée Bourdelle, which is in a part of the 15th arrondissement that's full of artists' workshops.

Where do you go to escape?

Granville, in Normandy, where our company Macon & Lesquoy is based. The beaches are sublime and deserted, the horizon is always present and the sky is different all the time. I also like to go to Ferrières-en-Gâtinais, in the Loiret; it's very close to Paris so it's good for when you don't have enough time to go further.

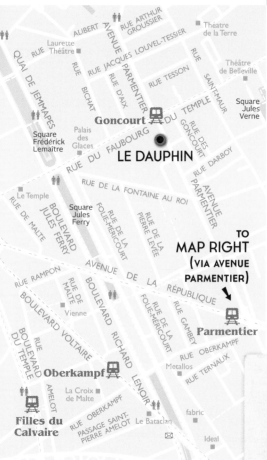

**TO
MAP RIGHT
(VIA AVENUE
PARMENTIER)**

The 11e, fanning out north-east of the Place de la Bastille, was once the preserve of small furniture factories and artisans' workshops, making for a refreshingly human-scaled neighbourhood. Its cheaper rents have drawn bohemian residents since the '80s and it's gone in and out of fashion several times since (currently it's definitely 'in').

Late-night action centres on rue Oberkampf, while down around rue de Charonne and along white-hot rue Amelot, the bar and dining scene has never been more vibrant. Shopping in this arrondissement is similarly switched on, with rue Charonne's major fashion names Isabel Marant and Sessun mixing it up with lots of little labels, independent makers and second-hand dealers.

24   JUN 8016

SHOP
1 ATELIER PMPM
2 FRENCH TROTTERS
3 LE CHOCOLAT ALAIN DUCASSE

EAT AND DRINK
4 QUI PLUME LA LUNE
5 CLAMATO

17

6 LE DAUPHIN
7 FOLKS & SPARROWS
8 SEPTIME & SEPTIME LA CAVE
9 CLOWN BAR
10 AU PASSAGE
11 LE PERCHOIR

DRINK
12 LE FANFARON

11E: BASTILLE, CHARONNE AND OBERKAMPF

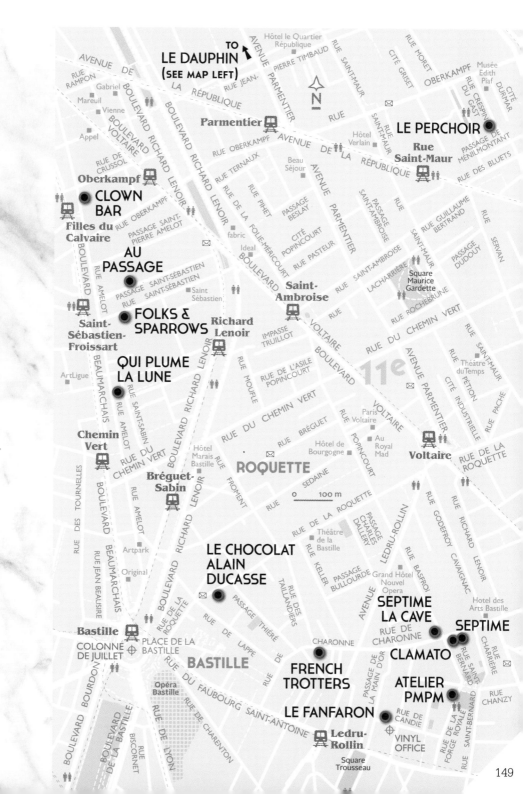

1.

ATELIER PMPM
27 rue de la Forge Royale
06 77 63 86 66
pmpm.fr
Open Tues–Sun 1–7pm
Metro: Faidherbe-Chaligny,
Ledru-Rollin

Marie Lautrou's tiny atelier is a genuine workshop – if you drop by you'll often find her hard at work at the pottery wheel or stacking the kiln. Her handcrafted stoneware platters, cups, vases and other vessels have a beautifully earthy 'back to nature' feel – one that's popping up more and more in Paris' bistros. Marie's background as a painter and her training in both the techniques and aesthetic values of Asian ceramics – where the mark of the artist's finger is seen as a thing of beauty, not something to be smoothed away – make her wares the real deal.

2.

FRENCH TROTTERS
30 rue de Charonne
01 47 00 84 35
frenchtrotters.fr
Open Mon 1.30–7.30pm,
Tues–Sat 11.30am–7.30pm
Metro: Ledru-Rollin

This bijou fashion superstore packs in an inspiring collection of labels, including clever picks from everyone's favourite Frenchies A.P.C. and Le Mont Saint Michel. Lesser-known designers are also represented, including Italian luxury deconstructionist Forte_ Forte, and then there's Michel Vivien, with his sublimely detailed ankle boots and disco-ready sandals. Owners Carole and Clarent Dehlouz design the women's and men's house label respectively. Their beautifully crafted, playful and earthy basics – think cropped quilted jackets, collarless shirts, and button-through sundresses – often carry over from season to season, but with fabrics and prints updated. Yes, these are forever clothes. There's a perfect selection of homewares, jewellery and accessories too.

3.

LE CHOCOLAT ALAIN DUCASSE

40 rue de la Roquette
01 48 05 82 86
lechocolat-alainducasse.com
Open Tues–Sat 10.30am–7pm
Metro: Bastille, Ledru-Rollin

A second-generation chocolatier-pâtissier, Nicolas Berger grew up counting bonbons. After long stints in chef Alain Ducasse's kitchens, he now heads up his boss' bean-to-bar 'manufacturing plant', the only one of its kind in Paris. This might possibly be the most photogenic factory on the planet, but one where some extraordinary things are also achieved. Watch while the team roasts, grinds, winnows and conches, then moulds the resulting chocolate into the ganaches, pralines and truffles that end up in Ducasse establishments around the world, and, more importantly, in the boxes you can buy to take home. Flavours like passionfruit, tonka bean, fresh mint and smoky coffee are utterly unforgettable.

4.

QUI PLUME LA LUNE
50 rue Amelot
01 48 07 45 48
quiplumelalune.fr
Open Wed–Sat 12–2.30pm
& 7–11pm
Metro: Chemin Vert,
Richard-Lenoir

If you're hankering for some Michelin-starred kitchen action but not the whole song and dance, Breton chef Jacky Ribault's unassuming little place might be right up your alley. The unusual fit-out, care of Ribault's wife, mixes wood, chrome, leather and stone with lambskins thrown across vintage chairs, tree branches and other organic elements. Ribault's cooking has Japanese influences that are often interwoven with classic French ingredients. A daily menu takes choice out of the equation: dinner is a set five-course deal, or choose between three to five courses at lunch. The wine – and beer – list features some notable organic and natural drops.

5.

CLAMATO

80 rue de Charonne
01 43 72 74 53
septime-charonne.fr
Open Wed–Fri 6–11pm,
Sat–Sun 11am–11pm
Metro: Ledru-Rollin, Charonne

With its upcycled cabin-style interior and catchy Americana moniker, Clamato could be all style and no substance. But no! Here you'll find some of the freshest and most pleasing seafood dishes this side of the Atlantic coast, along with queues of effortlessly stylish locals to prove it. Served by knowledgeable, friendly, multitasking staff, the small-plate menu gives plenty of scope to roam, from the familiar (raw plates simply spritzed with citrus) to the gently experimental (tiny Venus clams in a bath of fragrant elderflower broth). Boutique producer, mostly natural, wines are chosen to perfectly complement the dishes' delicate, nuanced flavours. No bookings are taken, but food is served nonstop on weekends, which means it's easier to nab a table either side of peak meal times.

6.

LE DAUPHIN

131 avenue Parmentier
01 55 28 78 88
restaurantledauphin.net
Open Tues–Sat 12–2pm &
7.30–11pm
Metro: Goncourt

At half a decade old (and that's *old* in neo-bistro years), Le Dauphin is still one of Paris' most striking restaurants. Dutch architect Rem Koolhaas' interior of moody grey marble and mirrors might sound a tad on the cold side, but the space is warmed by clusters of bentwood chairs and a soft glow from pillar candles. Tapas is the thing here, but not as you know it. This is Inaki Aizpitarte's casual option (the famed French-Basque chef's Le Chateaubriand is next door) and he plays on traditional, sometimes regional, French standards, like steak tartare, beef bourguignon and brandade. Dishes here are not just taste sensations; they're also often visual poems, topped with perfectly turned out tiny vegetables and rare leaves.

FOLKS & SPARROWS

14 rue Saint-Sébastien
09 81 45 90 99
Open Tues–Sun 10am–7pm
Metro: Saint-Sébastien-Froissart,
Richard-Lenoir

When visiting Folks &
Sparrows, you can never be
sure if Franck, the friendly,
bearded and be-hatted owner,
is spinning discs behind the
counter or stuffing baguettes
with Prince de Paris ham and
moutarde de Brive. Equally
equipped to cater for a fly-by
picnic run or a settle-in-for-
an-afternoon coffee marathon,
this is a joyful and welcoming
café, where wooden tables
are adorned with freshly-
plucked-from-a-meadow
flower arrangements. A lot
of love goes into the coffee
(made from the beans of Café
Lomi in the 18e) and little
lunch menu. Shelves are
stacked with a nice selection
of international deli goods –
all great-quality produce and
also lovely eye candy.

SEPTIME & SEPTIME LA CAVE

80 rue de Charonne (restaurant),
3 rue Basfroi (bar)
01 43 67 38 29 (restaurant),
01 43 67 14 87 (bar)
septime-charonne.fr
Open Mon 7.30–10pm,
Tues–Fri 12.15–2pm & 7.30–
10pm (restaurant); Tues–Sat
4–11pm (bar)
Metro: Ledru-Rollin, Charonne

Bertrand Grébaut's Septime
has been one of the hottest
tables in town for a few years
now. Online bookings are
released in three-week blocks
and are snapped up within
seconds. So is it worth the
fuss? Of course – the superb
five-course dinner menu is a
steal and the sweetly rustic
room is delightful. Grébaut
has an assured handle on
classical French technique
but is not afraid to play, and
he also serves up some of the
best produce in the city. If
you miss out (or even if you
don't), Septime's cellar bar
is a captivating consolation,
just around the corner.
Although the bar only serves
snacks, these are predictably
delicious, and the wine list,
quite fabulous.

PARIS TIP

There are but a few stones left of the historic Bastille prison fortress, but the roundabout on its site – topped with the Colonne de Juillet (July Column; *see map* p. 149) – is still the favoured setting for any form of Parisian protest.

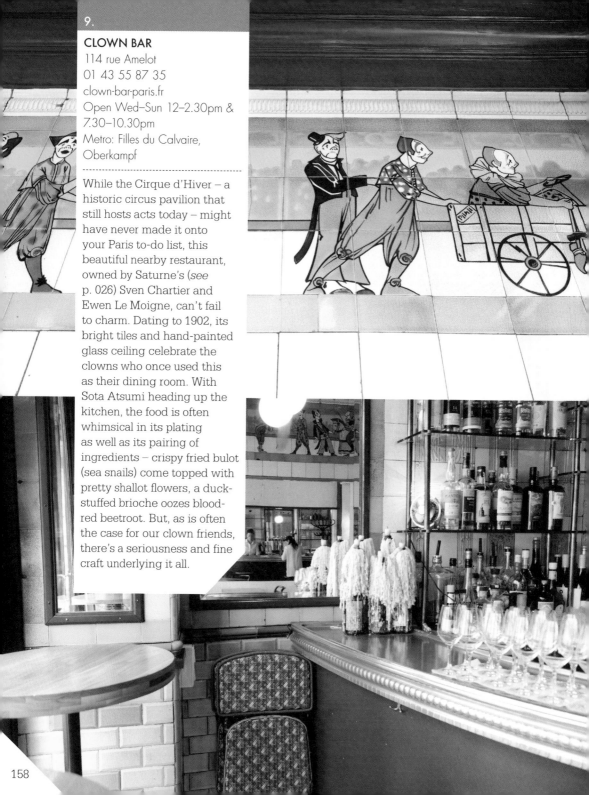

CLOWN BAR
114 rue Amelot
01 43 55 87 35
clown-bar-paris.fr
Open Wed–Sun 12–2.30pm &
7.30–10.30pm
Metro: Filles du Calvaire,
Oberkampf

While the Cirque d'Hiver – a
historic circus pavilion that
still hosts acts today – might
have never made it onto
your Paris to-do list, this
beautiful nearby restaurant,
owned by Saturne's (*see*
p. 026) Sven Chartier and
Ewen Le Moigne, can't fail
to charm. Dating to 1902, its
bright tiles and hand-painted
glass ceiling celebrate the
clowns who once used this
as their dining room. With
Sota Atsumi heading up the
kitchen, the food is often
whimsical in its plating
as well as its pairing of
ingredients – crispy fried bulot
(sea snails) come topped with
pretty shallot flowers, a duck-
stuffed brioche oozes blood-
red beetroot. But, as is often
the case for our clown friends,
there's a seriousness and fine
craft underlying it all.

AU PASSAGE

1bis passage Saint-Sébastien
01 43 55 07 52
restaurant-aupassage.fr
Open Mon–Sat 7pm–1.30am
Metro: Saint-Sébastien-Froissart,
Richard-Lenoir

- -

Englishman Ed Delling-Williams heads the kitchen at Au Passage – arrive a bit before 7pm to nab a place at the bar and you'll often find him hovering around the kitchen cubbyhouse chatting with his crew. The ramshackle interior, casually daubed chalkboard and often frenzied pace might seem a little out of step with this restaurant's lauded reputation. But don't be fooled – the food here is some of Paris' most innovative *and* honest cooking. Ephemeral one moment (a clear tomato broth topped with a lily-pond-like nasturtium leaf), hearty and homey another (spiced shoulder of lamb) and artful the next (snow crab topped with shards of burnt leek and crisped pig skin), it's also astonishingly good value.

11.

LE PERCHOIR
Levels 6 & 7, 14 rue Crespin
du Gast
01 48 06 18 48
leperchoir.fr
Open Mon–Fri 4pm–2am,
Sat–Sun 2pm–2am
Metro: Rue Saint-Maur,
Ménilmontant

The website of this terrace bar sums up its view perfectly: 'you will see birds, the Sacré-Cœur, chimneys, tomato plants'. Up on the 7th floor of an unmarked industrial building, this intoxicating mix of the everyday and the OMG can be had for 360 degrees. The crowd sharing bottles of rosé and cocktails du jour are not necessarily local, but the spirit is informal and fun. On the next floor down, the dramatically industrial restaurant is something of an insiders' secret – book ahead for great Provençal dishes served family style. If you're heading to the bar, arrive early (or very late) to avoid the queues – the seemingly vast rooftop reaches capacity quickly.

12.

LE FANFARON
6 rue de la Main d'Or
01 49 23 41 14
Open Mon–Sat 7pm–2am
Metro: Ledru-Rollin

Dino Risi's frantic existential road movie *Il Sorpasso* was renamed *Le Fanfaron* in French, and there's something of the film's slapstick intensity at this hidden-away namesake bar. Owner Xavier's got a tequila shot waiting for all comers, which usually includes the neighbourhood's artists, musicians and assorted misfits, but also the occasional model-slash-actress and a few up-for-it travellers. Painted a particularly evocative shade of deep, deep red and plastered with posters of Iggy Pop and the Only Ones, it's an easy space to sink into. Expect old vinyl on the turntable, the glow of candles that make everyone seem beautiful, and, at some point, dancing on the bar.

12.

11.

Gwen Jamois lives in the heart of the 11e near the Bastille. He runs a record label and is a composer of 'musique concrete' – a very French form of electronic music. He can be spotted wandering the Faubourg Saint-Antoine, rummaging through old book and record shops. His motto? 'Everyday is a muscadet.'

Which piece of music defines Paris for you?

There are so many, but the first that comes to mind is 'Le Poinçonneur des Lilas' by Serge Gainsbourg, a song about the lonely life of a Paris Metro ticket inspector slowly going mad. Or John Lewis and Sacha Distel's *Afternoon in Paris*, because Paris is a jazz city; it's a masterful LP, complete with a beautiful cover shot of John and Sacha walking on a misty morning, with the Eiffel Tower in the background.

What's a little known fact about the 11e?

This arrondissement has the highest alcohol consumption per square kilometre in the whole of France. It's a thirsty place.

What's your favourite shop?

It has to be Vinyl Office (*see map* p. 149), the finest second-hand record shop in Paris without a doubt. You never know what you're going to find there, from French exotica to eskimo jazz and yé-yé ['60s pop music] classics.

What's your favourite iconic Paris place?

The market of the place d'Aligre (*see* p. 166) has to be checked out; it's the oldest and best of the city. If you're there on a Sunday, go eat some oysters at Le Baron Rouge (*see* p. 172) and say bonjour to Christel the oyster queen.

What is the best place for a night out?

Check out Le Fanfaron (*see* p. 160), the most rock'n'roll bar in the world; Xavier the owner, barman and DJ is as crazy a Frenchman as they come.

Often given the city's 'most boring' arrondissement accolade, the young, fashionable families who've moved to the 12e over the last decade know better. Sharing the Bastille and rue du Faubourg Saint-Antoine with the 11e, the 12th's less-touristy expanses are home to one of the city's most vibrant produce markets, Marché d'Aligre (*see* p. 166), and lots of laid-back dining and drinking options.

Further south along the Seine is Bercy, where the city's wine was once warehoused; it's now a shopping village with cinemas, parks and a stadium. But the arrondissement's best-kept secret? The lush green corridor of the Coulée Verte, aka the Promenade Plantée, an elevated park on the old Vincennes railway viaduct.

Opéra Bastille

RUE DU FAUBOURG SAINT-ANTOINE

PASSAGE DE LA BOULE BLANCHE

COUR DU BEL AIR

RUE DE CHARENTON

PASSAGE DU CHANTIER

12e

QUINZE-VINGTS

Luxor Bastille

RUE MOREAU

RUE

RUE DE LYON

24   JUN 8016

*S*HOP
1 Caravane
*S*HOP **AND** EAT
2 Le Marché d'Aligre
EAT
3 Blé *S*ucré

EAT **AND** DRINK
4 Dersou
5 East Mamma
6 Le *S*quare Trousseau
7 Le Baron Rouge
8 Table

12E: ALIGRE, BERCY AND THE COULÉE VERTE

1.

CARAVANE
22 rue Saint-Nicolas
01 53 17 18 55
caravane.fr
Open Tues–Sat 11am–7pm
Metro: Ledru-Rollin, Bastille

Françoise Dorget, Caravane's original owner, pioneered the haute-hippy interior two decades ago. The Caravane empire – there are four other stores in Paris and one in London – is now in the trusted hands of Véronique and Jack-Eric Piedeleu. This little homewares shop, across the road from the Caravane furniture shop at no. 19, sells a range of distinctive treasures, destined to bring you years of daily pleasure. Porcelain, earthenware, wood and enamel bowls and plates of all proportions, beautifully crafted cutlery and serving implements, table and bed linen, and boldly patterned rugs and throws are sourced from small artisan operations. These hail from a travel addict's roll call of destinations, including India, Morocco, Nepal, West Africa and Eastern Europe.

2.

LE MARCHÉ D'ALIGRE
Place d'Aligre
01 45 11 71 11
marchedaligre.free.fr
Open Tues–Sun 9am–12.30pm
(outdoor stalls); Tues–Sat
9am–12.30pm & 4–7.30pm,
Sun 9am–12.30pm
(Marché Beauvau)
Metro: Ledru-Rollin, Bastille

Although you'll never be far from a Franprix, Monoprix or Carrefour supermarket in Paris, it remains a city of beloved neighbourhood markets. Marché d'Aligre might not offer postcard views or poshly packaged produce, but it is one of the city's most vibrant and varied markets, selling fruit, vegetables and flowers from sprawling outside stalls. At its centre, the covered **Marché Beauvau** offers more of the same, as well as game, charcuterie, cheese and seafood. On the curving sweep of the Place d'Aligre, beside the Marché Beauvau, there are brocante stalls too, specialising variously in books, CDs, ceramics, paintings, and traditional masks and sculptures from the Côte d'Ivoire – along with some plain-old fabulous French junk.

1.

2.

2.

1.

1.

2.

3.

BLÉ SUCRÉ

7 rue Antoine Vollon
01 43 40 77 73
Open Tues–Sat 7.30am–7.30pm,
Sun 7am–1.30pm
Metro: Ledru-Rollin

Across from a beautiful leafy square, Blé Sucré is the kind of neighbourhood patisserie that makes you *really* wish you lived in the neighbourhood. Fabrice Le Bourdat, former pâtissier of the prestigious Plaza Athénée and Hotel Bristol, produces croissants, viennoiserie (pastries) and tarte au citron that regularly make the 'best' lists of national newspaper *Le Figaro*. Bourdat's creations will make traditionalists smile: they're perfect, straight-down-the-line models with no fusion ingredients or witty twists. That said, his madeleines *are* a tad different, as well as exceptional. A subtle innovation – the little cakes are painted with an orange glaze post-baking – makes them possibly the moistest and most delicate in all of Paris.

DERSOU

21 rue Saint-Nicolas
09 81 01 12 73
dersouparis.com
Open Tues–Fri 7pm–12am,
Sat 12–3.30pm & 7.30pm–
12.30am, Sun 12–4pm
Metro: Ledru-Rollin, Bastille

There's a rawness to the
stripped-back walls and open
kitchen at this high-ceilinged
shopfront restaurant, but
also a beautiful tactility and
warmth, with tables made
from recycled Belgian wood
and stacks of service-ready
artisan-made ceramics.
Alain Ducasse–trained Taku
Sekine's cooking is a global,
often Asian, mix, similarly
earthy and stripped back, but
also rather finessed. Simple,
herb-strewn dishes are
served at Saturday lunch and
Sunday brunch (pancakes and
avocado toast also turn up on
the brunch menu). Bookings
are taken for the first dinner
sitting – a fancier five-course,
five-matched-cocktails deal
(yes, *five* matched cocktails,
care of star bartender Amaury
Guyot), or come later for
à la carte, with last orders
at midnight.

5.

EAST MAMMA
133 rue du Faubourg Saint-Antoine
01 43 41 32 15
bigmammagroup.com
Open Mon–Sun 12.15–2.45pm
& 7.30–11pm
Metro: Ledru-Rollin

Paris is in the throes of a transalpine culinary crush, with burrata cheese, ravioli and the Italian aperitif Aperol currently must-haves all over town. East Mamma may call itself a 'trattoria populare' – a common people's trattoria – but it's more of a distillation of the most fashionable elements of the Italian kitchen, something that makes it populare indeed. Produce is the star here and the placemat menus proudly list the provenance of all, much of it 'bio' (organic). At lunch or dinner, you can chow down on puffy, impressively charred Neapolitan-style pizzas, perfect homemade pasta, roasts or osso bucco, and all can be washed down with great regional wines from across Italy.

6.

LE SQUARE TROUSSEAU
1 rue Antoine Vollon
01 43 43 06 00
squaretrousseau.com
Open Mon–Sun 8am–2am
Metro: Ledru-Rollin

The huge, heated terrace and square-side locale are reason enough to love this place, but its 1910 interior is even more endearing. The archetypal Belle Époque decor is highly cinematic, and is a favourite of French film directors, finding its way into several films, including *Paris, Je T'Aime*. Mornings dawn with pastries from nearby Blé Sucré (*see* p. 168) or omelettes done many ways. After that, the menu remains traditional (slow-cooked lamb, house-made duck terrine), but makes a few contemporary concessions (burgers, risotto) and is served continuously from noon to midnight – perfect if you're ravenous after an afternoon shopping binge on nearby rue du Faubourg Saint-Antoine.

5.

6.

6.

5.

5.

6.

7.

LE BARON ROUGE
1 rue Théophile Roussel
01 43 43 14 32
Open Mon 5–10pm, Tues–Fri
10am–2pm & 5–10pm, Sat
10am–10pm, Sun 10am–4pm
Metro: Ledru-Rollin, Bastille

Here's sweet succour for those who are tired of high concepts on one hand, and low-quality food and wine on the other. Le Baron Rouge manages to tread the tightrope of actually being a local Parisian bar while at the same time fulfilling the fantasy of one. Tourists come for a peek, some even stay, but the good, and very cheap, wines keep flowing regardless, the soundtrack, care of moonlighting musician and DJ bartenders, is never dull and the eccentric bonhomie is seemingly eternal. And, yes, it's perfectly acceptable to quaff a muscadet at the original zinc bar at 11am, and absolutely no problem if you're still here at closing. Stomach-lining snacks include freshly shucked oysters in season, well-chosen charcuterie and cheese year-round.

PARIS TIP
The Coulée Verte was the world's first elevated park. After a 4.5 kilometre verdant adventure of rooftop views among roses, lavender, wisteria, vines and bamboo, a further 1.5 kilometre street-level (and bikeable) stretch continues to the Bois de Vincennes gardens.

TABLE

3 rue de Prague
01 43 43 12 26
tablerestaurant.fr
Open Mon–Fri lunch & dinner
Metro: Ledru-Rollin

Food writer, cookbook author and radio personality Bruno Verjus has created a theatrically masculine, strangely sensual space at his restaurant Table. The interior is dimly lit and dominated by a big curving pewter bar where diners sit together enthralled by all the cheffy action (including Verjus himself) in the open kitchen. Whatever's on the super-short menu – rouget (red mullet), morels, suckling lamb, roast beef on the bone, Beninese pineapple or chocolate mousse – is best-of-breed, simply plated and paired with one or two vegetable, herb or aromatic elements. Table's up-there pricing can be polarising: go regardless if you're a fine-produce buff, or otherwise test the waters with the very well priced daily lunch menu.

Daran, an expat Australian, is a production designer, with film credits including *The Bourne Identity*, *Blood Diamond* and *Samson & Delilah*. He's worked around the world from Cape Town and Dublin to Dubai, Maputo and Prague, and has been based in Paris for over 15 years. He is set to launch his first range of 3D printed jewellery.

Where do you find inspiration?

In Paris lots of my inspiration comes from walking and wandering the streets. The scale of the city is very human, so I try to walk as much as possible instead of catching public transport or driving. I love discovering the rich, old and varied architecture of the city and how it combines with Paris' inhabitants and the ever-present modern graffiti.

What is your favourite place to hang out in the 12e?

I like to head to Lake Daumesnil on weekends for a breath of fresh air; it's great for a walk, picnic or bike ride. I also love going to the popular Marché d'Aligre (*see* p. 166) for its large fresh selection and village atmosphere; with all ages

bustling in the crowded street, it can feel a little like something out of *Oliver Twist*.

What's your favourite iconic Paris moment?

I love walking around during the annual Fête de la Musique on 21 June, when the whole city explodes with impromptu midsummer concerts. Fête de la Musique regulars here include a big brass band of 40 or so members, reggae DJs who use a grandma's watercolour shop as a base, and a blues band that takes over an entire pizza restaurant while its audience watches from the street. It's a Fellini-esque evening with music emanating from shops, cafes, windows and rooftops, all blending, competing and complementing, and resonating all over Paris at the same time.

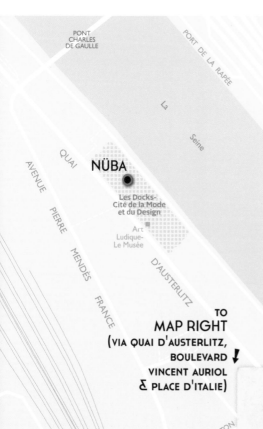

PONT
CHARLES
DE GAULLE

PORT DE LA RAPÉE

La
Seine

QUAI

AVENUE

PIERRE

MENDÈS

FRANCE

D'AUSTERLITZ

NÜBA

Les Docks-
Cité de la Mode
et du Design

Art
Ludique-
Le Musée

TO
MAP RIGHT
(VIA QUAI D'AUSTERLITZ,
BOULEVARD
VINCENT AURIOL
& PLACE D'ITALIE)

RUE FULTON

The wide, wide boulevards of Gobelins and much of this sprawling arrondissement can make you feel like you're no longer in Paris. Then, tucked away just behind the shopping malls, cinemas and office blocks of the Place d'Italie, there's the Butte-aux-Cailles.

This village-like enclave of cobbled streets and ivy-clad townhouses is known for its boisterous bars and cheap restaurants and, along with the nearby Asian Quarter, is a perennial favourite of the area's large student population. Students also find their way to the Seine-side Quai d'Austerlitz, where young and beautiful Parisians come for the party boats, a summer 'beach' and pool, and year-round bars, clubs and restaurants.

24   JUN 80T6

SHOP
1   LES ABEILLES
EAT
2   L'AVANT GOÛT

17

EAT AND DRINK
3   L'OURCINE
4   SIMONE RESTAURANT & BAR
DRINK
5   NÜBA
6   LE MERLE MOQUEUR

13E: PLACE D'ITALIE, GOBELINS AND QUAI D'AUSTERLITZ

L'OURCINE

SIMONE
RESTAURANT
& BAR

HOTEL
HENRIETTE

Les
Gobelins

RUE SAINT-HIPPOLYTE

RUE BROCA

RUE SAINT-HIPPOLYTE

RUE PASCAL

BOULEVARD ARAGO

BOULEVARD ARAGO

RUE DES

RUE DE LA
REINE BLANCHE

RUE NICOLAS ROBERT

RUE BROCA

RUE BERBIER-DU-METS

RUE ÉMILE DESLANDRES

RUE DE JULIENNE

Hôtel
Belambra
Magendie

RUE PASCAL

RUE DES TANNERIES

RUE CORVISART

RUE DES

CORDELIÈRES

RUE GUSTAVE GEFFROY

Galerie
des
Gobelins

RUE LE BRUN

RUE DE CROULEBARBE

GOBELINS

RUE DU
BANQUIER

VILLA DES
GOBELINS

RUE ABEL HOVELACQUE

RUE VÉRONÈSE

AVENUE DES

AVENUE DES GOBELINS

Mobilier
National

RUE BERBIER-DU-METS

LES
GOBELINS

N

RUE DU CHAMP
DE L'ALOUETTE

RUE VULPIAN

RUE CORVISART

GERVAIS

RUE PAUL

Square
René Le Gall

DE

CROULEBARBE

RUE

DES

RECULETTES

Mercure
Gobelins

AVENUE
DE LA SŒUR
ROSALIE

PLACE
D'ITALIE

13e

RUE EDMOND
GONDINET

RUE CORVISART

BOULEVARD

AUGUSTE

BLANQUI

RUE ABEL HOVELACQUE

TO
NÜBA
(SEE MAP
LEFT)

0   100 m

RUE DU PÈRE GUÉRIN

Citadines
Place
d'Italie

BOULEVARD

AUGUSTE BLANQUI

RUE LE DANTEC

RUE VERGNIAUD

RUE BARRAULT

PASSAGE BARRAULT

Corvisart

BUTTE-
AUX-CAILLES

DIAMANTS

CINQ

RUE GÉRARD

RUE DU MOULIN-DES-PRÉS

RUE
PAULIN MERY

RUE BOBILLOT

RUE LE
DANTEC

Timhotel
Place
d'Italie

RUE ALPHAND

Jardin
Brassaï

RUE

DES

RUE SAMSON

RUE SIMONET

L'AVANT
GOÛT

PASSAGE
SIGAUD

LES
ABEILLES

LE MERLE
MOQUEUR

RUE JEAN-
MARIE JÉGO

RUE DE LA BUTTE
AUX CAILLES

RUE DE LA
BUTTE-AUX-CAILLES

Square
Henri-
Rousselle

RUE CHÉREAU

PLACE
PAUL
VERLAINE

RUE DU MOULIN-DES-PRÉS

RUE BOBILLOT

VILLA DAVIEL

RUE MICHAL

RUE BUOT

Hôtel
Saint-Charles

PASSAGE
BOTON

RUE DE POUY

1.

LES ABEILLES
21 rue de la Butte-aux-Cailles
01 45 81 43 48
lesabeilles.biz
Open Tues–Sat 11am–7pm
Metro: Corvisart

The name of this precious, tiny shop means 'the bees', and the burly beekeeper in charge sells absolutely everything that's bee related. You might not be in the market for tools of the apiarist trade, of which there are many, but there's an astounding range of the edible, medicinal and utilitarian: beeswax candles and healing honey skincare, jars of the sweet stuff scented with a huge range of flowers and leaves, and honey-flavoured products such as mustard and vinegar. Don't miss the baked goods – sticky little orange-scented nonnette cakes and slabs of pain d'épice (a dense, spiced honey loaf).

2.

L'AVANT GOÛT
26 rue Bobillot
01 53 80 24 00
lavantgout.com
Open Tues–Sat 12–2pm &
7.30–10pm
Metro: Corvisart, Place d'Italie

The sweet cartoon mural of plump pigs a-frolicking might give you a wee hint as to what chef Christophe Beaufront's speciality is. Pork, yes, but specifically pot-au-feu de cochon aux épices – pork done in a quintessentially French long-simmered stew, usually reserved for beef (he also turns out a popular dish of crumbed, roast pig trotters). His incredibly well-priced menus and à la carte dishes also cater for more delicate appetites, with dishes like ravioli of duck, chicken terrine with escargot and almonds, and market-fresh fish in Asian-spiced broths. While there's a neo-bistro sensibility to the food, don't expect high concepts or magazine-worthy decor, instead both are as idiosyncratic as they are heartfelt.

The BnF (Bibliothèque nationale de France) is one of the world's largest libraries. Check out its interesting contemporary architecture, excellent and crowd-free exhibitions along with a glimpse of French student life.

1.

2.

3.

L'OURCINE

92 rue Broca
01 47 07 13 65
restaurant-lourcine.fr
Open Tues–Sat 12–2.30pm &
7–11pm
Metro: Les Gobelins

There's a very traditional look
and feel to this bistro (you
may even need to practise
your French), but the dishes
that emerge from the kitchen
as part of either the lunch
or evening prix fixe menu
(both good value), are in
fact, delightfully inventive
and seasonally attuned. The
'supplements' – surcharges
over and above the menu
price – on many dishes are
a clue to the high-calibre
produce used (say partridge,
abalone or Corsican raw
cheese). The wine selection,
too, is a surprise, with unusual
choices from small producers,
many of which can be had
by the glass or the demi
(500 millilitre) jug.

SIMONE RESTAURANT & BAR

33 boulevard Arago (restaurant),
48 rue Pascal (bar)
01 43 37 82 70
simoneparis.com
Open Tues–Fri 12–10pm,
Sat sittings 7.30pm & 9.30pm
(restaurant); Tues–Fri 4.30–8pm,
Sat 10.30am–8.30pm (bar)
Metro: Les Gobelins

A courtyard joins this restaurant-wine-bar duo, a pared-back but also spruced-up neighbourhood bistro that's something of an outlier in a sleepy residential stretch. Stellar natural wines feature in the restaurant, and the neat little wine bar has an even more extensive selection of cultish drops. The menu makes use of interesting ingredients (bergamot, kale, sweetbread, chestnuts), often in ambitious combinations, but is far from pretentious; similarly the service is enthusiastic, clued-up and accommodating. Everyone, whether they're settling in for the evening or just popping in for a bon verre du vin – that mythical 'one' good glass of wine – seems super pleased to be here.

NÜBA

36 Quai d'Austerlitz
01 76 77 34 85
lenuba.com
Open Tues–Sat 12–3pm &
6pm–5am, Sun 12pm–2am
Metro: Gare d'Austerlitz,
Quai de la Gare

When legendary club impresarios Lionel Bensemoun and Jean-Marie Tassy are behind a venture, you can count on some excellent late-night action. This rooftop eyrie, part of the waterfront Le Docks, aka Cité de la Mode et du Design (home to the French Institute of Fashion campus), hosts live music, dance shows and DJ sets. Unlike a lot of Paris' clubs, it's far from elitist, and in the warmer months takes on a beach-club vibe, even though there's not a grain of imported sand in sight. There are some gorgeous far-from-the-madding-crowd views along the Seine from here, and, although the food is far from notable, it's also a great sun's-out lunch spot.

LE MERLE MOQUEUR

11 rue de la Butte-aux-Cailles
Open Mon–Sun 5pm–2am
Metro: Corvisart, Place d'Italie

The bars of the Butte-aux-Cailles neighbourhood are a favourite with students from the many Left Bank seats of learning, and, as student bars often do, tend towards the messy. Finding a favourite is usually best accomplished by a little exploratory wander, ticking off music selection and crowd against your mood at the time. If you want a sure bet in the lively stakes, Le Merle Moqueur will deliver, due in part to its impressive selection of rum. Grab a Ti' Punch (rum with lime juice and sugar) and go outside with your new-found friends if the '80s tunes are not to your taste, or wait for the ramped-up pop classics – singalong time.

Vanessa is a fashion editor and stylist turned interior designer and hotelier. Her latest project, Gobelins' Hotel Henriette (*see map* p. 177), encapsulates her particular style, with a charming mix of vintage pieces, cleverly used textiles and rock'n'roll detail.

How would you define contemporary Parisian style?

It's impossible to define! In Paris there will always be a certain je ne sais quoi [a quality that can't be easily described].

What are your favourite places in the 13e?

The beautiful rooftop at Nüba (*see* p. 182), the streets of the Butte-aux-Cailles neighbourhood, and Manufacture des Gobelins, 17th-century tapestry workshops that are a museum but also still in use.

What do you love about the 13e?

It's historically and culturally very rich. But it's also a very green district, and there are so many little gardens hidden everywhere; it's nice to try to discover them while walking around the neighbourhood.

Where do you go to escape?

It's always nice to go to Versailles and walk through the park. I also love Le Perche in lower Normandy – it's only two hours away and is so beautiful!

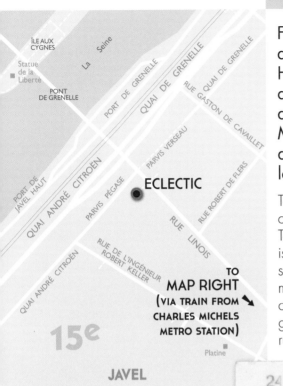

ÎLE AUX CYGNES
Statue de la Liberté
PONT DE GRENELLE

La Seine

QUAI DE GRENELLE

RUE QUAI DE GRENELLE

PORT DE GRENELLE

RUE GASTON DE CAVAILLET

PARVIS VERSEAU

RUE ROBERT DE FLERS

PORT DE JAVEL HAUT

QUAI ANDRÉ CITROEN

PARVIS PÉGASE

ECLECTIC

RUE LINOIS

RUE DE L'INGÉNIEUR ROBERT KELLER

QUAI ANDRÉ CITROEN

15e

TO
MAP RIGHT
(VIA TRAIN FROM
CHARLES MICHELS
METRO STATION)

Platine

JAVEL

RUE DE JAVEL

AVENUE ÉMILE ZOLA

Fabled Montparnasse spans both of these arrondissements and was once home to Hemingway, Picasso, Chagall and even a young Lenin. Le Dôme, La Rotonde and La Coupole, the cafés where these Montparnassions wrote, fought, flirted and often slept are still in business, if no longer a picture of bohemian excess.

Today this is a resolutely family oriented part of the city, with laid-back dining and drinking scenes. The Tour Montparnasse – the tallest skyscraper in Paris – is an unavoidable landmark, as is the hulking train station, Gare Montparnasse. Rail links to Brittany made this area a Breton stronghold, hence the jolly creperies that dole out authentic Breton buckwheat galettes around rue du Montparnasse and rue Delambre.

24   JUN 80T6

EAT
1   HEXAGONE CAFÉ
EAT AND DRINK
2   LA CANTINE DU TROQUET DAGUERRE

17

EAT AND DRINK (CONT.)
3 CIEL DE PARIS
4 MONTPARNASSE 1900
5 ECLECTIC

14E AND 15E: MONTPARNASSE

1.

HEXAGONE CAFÉ

121 rue du Château, 14e
hexagone-cafe.fr
Open Mon–Fri 8am–6pm,
Sat–Sun 10am–6pm
Metro: Pernety

Chung-Leng Tran, an award-winning barista from Fragments (*see* p. 047), espresso machine expert David Lahoz, barista trainer and coffee blogger Sébastien Racineux, and legendary Breton-based roaster Stéphane Cataldi decided to bring speciality coffee culture to this typical Parisian neighbourhood, and in so doing, quash the idea that 'good' coffee is but an Anglo indulgence. Hexagone – a nod to a term the French often use to describe France – is a large, whitewashed space with artisan wood benches and old classroom furniture. Join the locals who come here to work or watch the world go by with a café noisette (macchiato) and homemade pastry or a simple tartine – if you're lucky, Cataldi may have brought in honey from his own hives for these. Espressos are cranked out on a shiny, classic La Marzocco Linea PB, while the filter coffee is done on an aeropress.

2.

LA CANTINE DU TROQUET DAGUERRE

89 rue Daguerre, 14e
01 43 20 20 09
facebook.com/
lacantinedaguerre
Open Mon–Sun 12–2.30pm &
7–10.45pm
Metro: Denfert, Gaîté

Christian Etchebest, a genial TV chef from the south-west of France, has forged a mini-empire in the 14e and 15e. This is the most intimate of his trio of Cantine restaurants in the area, and its trad tiles and dark wood are a great fit for his sincere Basque cooking. Etchebest signature dishes such as crispy pig ears, griddle-seared razor clams, Atlantic whelks or cockles with celery remoulade, and melty lamb navarin stew make an appearance, along with seasonal specials and wonderful south-west wines. Come for oeufs mayo (hard-boiled eggs with mayonnaise) at the atmospheric zinc bar if you're in need of a rugby chat with Etchebest's regular crew of homesick south-westerners, or bring an appetite and keep on ploughing through till you reach the riz au lait caramel laitier (caramel rice pudding).

3.

CIEL DE PARIS

Level 56, Tour Maine
Montparnasse, 33 avenue du
Maine, 15e
01 40 64 77 64
cieldeparis.com
Open Mon–Sun 8.30–11am,
12–2.15pm & 7–11pm
Metro: Montparnasse-Bienvenüe

Let's get a few things straight.
This is a restaurant-with-a-
view and this is Paris. There
will be lots of tourists. And
the modern bistro food will
not be innovative or edgy.
Still, the Ciel's set menus are
'correct' (as the French say),
the staff are sweet, there's a
sexy original '70s interior and,
yes, that view. Yes, the view
is what you're really after,
so nab a window table just
after lunch or before dinner:
wine and Champagne by the
glass are well priced, a little
dish of freshly baked cheese
biscuits will appear at your
table and you can nibble,
sip and cloud-gaze to your
heart's content.

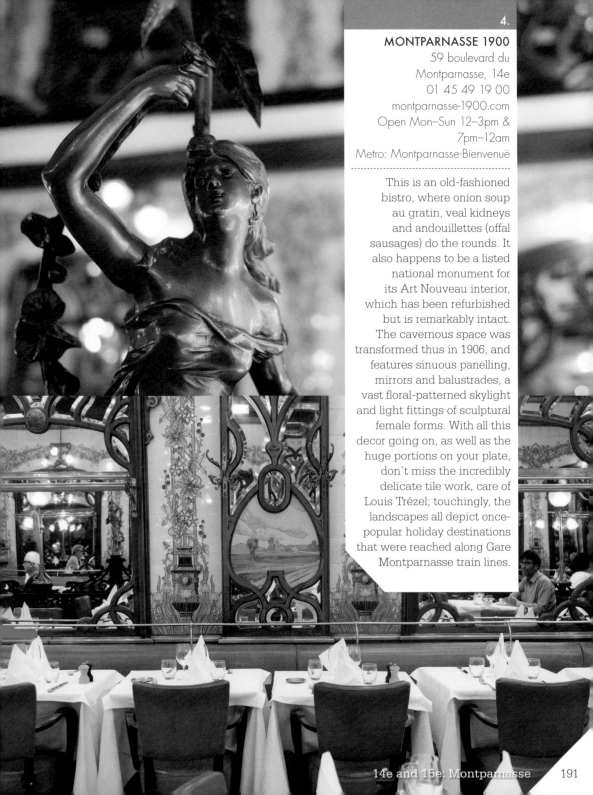

MONTPARNASSE 1900
59 boulevard du
Montparnasse, 14e
01 45 49 19 00
montparnasse-1900.com
Open Mon–Sun 12–3pm &
7pm–12am
Metro: Montparnasse-Bienvenuë

This is an old-fashioned bistro, where onion soup au gratin, veal kidneys and andouillettes (offal sausages) do the rounds. It also happens to be a listed national monument for its Art Nouveau interior, which has been refurbished but is remarkably intact. The cavernous space was transformed thus in 1906, and features sinuous panelling, mirrors and balustrades, a vast floral-patterned skylight and light fittings of sculptural female forms. With all this decor going on, as well as the huge portions on your plate, don't miss the incredibly delicate tile work, care of Louis Trézel; touchingly, the landscapes all depict once-popular holiday destinations that were reached along Gare Montparnasse train lines.

5.

ECLECTIC

2 rue Linois, 15e
01 77 36 70 00
restauranteclectic.fr
Open Mon–Sun 8am–12am
Metro: Charles Michels

The '70s Brutalism of the Beaugrenelle shopping mall earned it the nickname Mochegrenelle (moche meaning 'ugly') back in the day, but it was given a flash, futuristic makeover a couple of years ago. English designer Tom Dixon's Eclectic restaurant on the ground floor is both homage and departure from that austere architectural moment, exposing the concrete structure but filling it with his very-now mix of patterns and textures: brass panels, exquisitely rippled marble tabletops and a central chandelier made from 124 of his Cell lights. Join ladies who lunch and media boys who bistro for wide Seine views and pristinely presented classics – croque-monsieur and Bellini cocktail breakfasts, crab cakes and endive salad at lunch, kir royales (Champagne and cassis) and entrecôte steak with herbed butter for dinner.

PARIS TIP
Fondation Henri Cartier-Bresson (*see map* p. 187) houses the archive of the iconic photographer and wife Martine Franck in a restored 1912 artists' atelier, while the Fondation Henri Cartier-Bresson (*see map* p. 193) specialises in artworks from the 1980s onwards. Both are excellent and crowd free.

Chung-Leng is co-owner of Hexagone (*see* p. 188). He's previously been behind the coffee machines at Fragments (*see* p. 047) and Télescope (*see* p. 010), and was the 2012 French Brewer's Cup champion. He became a barista after a background in sociology, ethnology and photography.

How would you define contemporary Parisian style?

'I ♥ rien, I'm Parisien' (rien means 'nothing', and it's almost the truth).

Where else in Paris do you go for coffee?

When I have time, I like to drink coffee at Télescope, Fragments or Matamata in the 2e (*see map* p. 019).

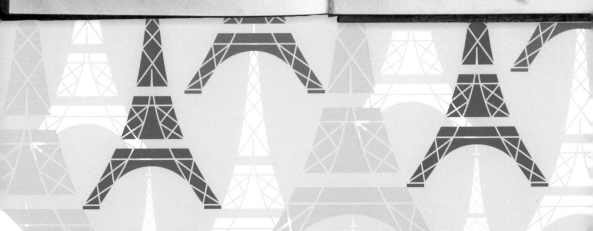

What's your favourite iconic Paris moment?

I love walking or cycling in Paris on 15 August, the big public holiday, because the city is empty. This is the only day of the year when the streets are deserted – it's unique and a great feeling.

Where do you go to escape?

Ouessant, a wild and beautiful island in Brittany. It's one of my favourite places in France, far away from Paris, but totally worth the trip.

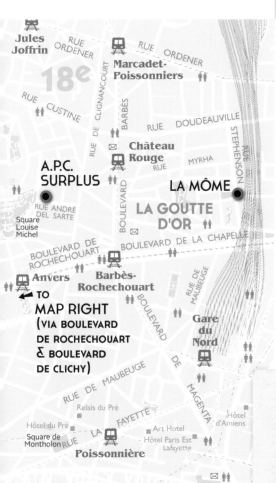

Topped by the ghostly dome of Sacré-Cœur basilica, Montmartre is crisscrossed by vertiginous cobbled streets, secret staircases and big, wide views. Artists of all persuasions, including Modigliani, Van Gogh and Erik Satie, were lured here by cheap rents and its bawdy dance halls at the end of the 19th century.

While the tourist tat at place du Tertre makes for a sad simulacrum of those bohemian days, a new breed of 'creative class' now favours Montmartre's slopes and neighbouring Batignolles. To the east of the 'Butte' – Sacré-Cœur's hill – is one of Paris' most culturally diverse areas. Barbès and nearby Château Rouge and Goutte d'Or have large West and North African communities, as well as a growing number of hipster-anointed bars.

17E AND 18E: MONTMARTRE, BATIGNOLLES AND BARBÈS

24   JUN 8076

SHOP
1 L'OBJET QUI PARLE
2 A.P.C. SURPLUS
3 CORPUS CHRISTI

SHOP, EAT AND DRINK
4 LE BAL CAFÉ & BOOKSHOP

EAT
5 CAFÉ TABAC

17

EAT AND DRINK
6 GARE AU GORILLE
7 LA MÔME

DRINK
8 CHEZ CAMILLE
9 LE TRÈS PARTICULIER

197

1.

L'OBJET QUI PARLE
86 rue des Martyrs, 18e
Open Mon–Sat 1.30–7.30pm
Metro: Abbesses, Pigalle

No time to trawl the Marché Saint-Ouen flea market? Head to this hole-in-the-wall favourite of Parisian art directors and set designers, where a veteran collector with a superbly idiosyncratic eye has already done the hard yards. The pieces at this brocante store murmur, sing and sometimes shout their intriguing back stories: naive portraits of infantrymen daubed on the Belgian front and 1920s vaudeville masks the size of lampshades hover over cabinets of religious artefacts and fittings from long-demolished hotels. Your decorating tastes tend more to Provençal pretty than dada dreamscape? No problem! There's also a large stock of well-priced, easily packed vintage porcelain, glassware and linen.

2.

A.P.C. SURPLUS
20 rue André del Sarte, 18e
01 42 62 10 88
apc.fr
Open Mon–Sat 12–7.30pm
Metro: Château Rouge,
Barbès-Rochechouart

- -

Jean Touitou's A.P.C., a
cultish Parisian label that's
totally cornered the bookishly
sexy market, makes the kind
of timeless clothes where
past seasons' stock can be
the main draw rather than
a short straw. Racks at this
surplus store are arranged by
colour, so have a flip through
for the shirts, smocks, frocks
and jackets that you fell in
love with a few seasons
back but by fate or restraint
never found their way into
your wardrobe. Discounts
hover between 40 and 60 per
cent off. Undiscounted key
pieces are also stocked,
such as home fragrances,
jeans and the house quilts
made from leftover dress and
shirt fabric.

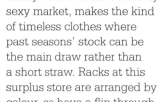

PARIS TIP
Over the boulevard
Périphérique, in the 18e's
far north, Marché aux
Puces de Saint-Ouen (aka
Clignancourt) is the most
famous of the Parisian flea
markets and one of the
world's largest. A rambling
self-contained village, it's
home to over 2000 stalls
and shops.

3.

CORPUS CHRISTI

6 rue Ravignan, 18e
01 42 57 77 77
corpuschristi.fr
Open Tues–Sat 11.30am–
7.30pm, Sun 1.30–7.30pm
Metro: Abbesses, Pigalle

Intriguing window displays
will pull you into this equally
intriguing jewellery shop,
where bracelets, rings,
necklaces and earrings for
both men and women hang
from deer horns or sit beneath
specimen domes. Designer
Thierry Gougenot, a one-
time painter, is inspired
by Baroque architecture,
rock'n'roll, sacred art and
tribal decoration, and his
work eschews trends.
Rather he draws on religious
iconography and there's a
delicate Gothic edge to his
crosses, articulated skeletons,
reliquaries, orbs, flowers
and feathers. The pieces are
crafted with sterling silver,
22-carat gold vermeil, pearls
and semiprecious stones, and
sit at a price point between
costume and fine jewellery –
perfect Parisian present-to-
self fodder.

LE BAL CAFÉ & BOOKSHOP
6 Impasse de la Défense, 18e
01 44 70 75 51 (café),
01 44 70 75 56 (bookshop)
le-bal.fr
Open Wed–Fri 12–11pm,
Sat 11am–11pm, Sun 11am–7pm
(café); Wed, Fri & Sat 12–8pm,
Thurs 12–10pm, Sun 12–7pm
(bookshop)
Metro: Place de Clichy

Venture up past the cray-cray of Place de Clichy to this hidden away gallery, café and bookshop, set in a 1920s dance hall/bordello. With the gallery specialising in contemporary photographic work, the attached bookshop is stocked with photography titles, non-mainstream films, works of theory and a range of international magazines. Head into the light-filled, garden-facing café, where Rose Bakery (*see* p. 118) alumni Anna Trattles and Alice Quillet concoct comforting, flavourful Anglo-French dishes, like kedgeree, pork and prune terrine or lamb chops with a herbed lentil salad. It's a perfect spot for lunch or Sunday brunch, but also rather nice for a low-key dinner. There's good coffee too, care of Anselme Blayney, a partner in local speciality roaster Belleville Brûlerie; team it with teatime treats like lemon-drizzle cake or peach frangipane tart.

5.

CAFÉ TABAC

1 rue Ravignan, 18e
01 42 51 44 53
Open Mon 8.30am–2pm,
Tues–Fri 8.30am–6pm, Sat–Sun
9am–6.30pm
Metro: Abbesses, Pigalle

On a cinematic corner,
Franco-Australian couple
Frédéric and Charlotte
Monnier have conjured up
a little bit of Melbourne in
Montmartre. Bucking the
speciality coffee trend,
Fred turns out perfect flat
whites and espressos using
Genovese beans, a veteran
Italian-Australian coffee
roaster. Charlotte's interior
of red Tolix stools, geometric
floor tiles and a stunning
mid-century chandelier is a
happy-making backdrop for
the café's steady stream of
regulars – freelancers popping
in for a chat and a Gontran
Cherrier croissant, parents
feeding cute kids jam tartines
(open sandwiches), and a few
caffeine-addicted locals who
seem quite content to stay
all day.

GARE AU GORILLE

68 rue des Dames, 17e
01 42 94 24 02
Open Tues–Sat 12.15–2.30pm
& 7.30–10pm
Metro: Rome, Place de Clichy

A smartly nonchalant fit-out of white tiles, old chairs and industrial lighting makes this little neo-bistro an immediately appealing place to be, but it's the food that draws gourmets from all over Paris. Young co-owner Marc Cordonnier got his chef chops at l'Arpege (*see* p. 094) and he and front-of-house partner Louis Langevin later worked at Septime (*see* p. 156). Dishes bear the hallmarks of Cordonnier's fine dining background but are never fussy or overworked. The menu also has a nice flexibility: you can either order a number of small plates – beautiful raw fish dishes, duck terrine, salt cod croquettes, baby vegetables – or take one as an entree and share one of the large, hearty meat options as a main.

7.

LA MÔME

16 rue Stephenson, 18e
01 42 23 35 64
Open Mon–Sat 12–3pm &
7–10.30pm
Metro: La Chapelle,
Château Rouge

A sign of the gentrifying times, the terrace of this Moroccan restaurant up in the 18e's Goutte d'Or often feels like a hipster house party. Old maps, '70s wallpaper and brocante furniture continue the theme inside, but the menu is a direct homage to the neighbourhood's North African community. The two sisters in the kitchen (also the owners) send out hearty Moroccan tagines – lamb and prunes, chicken with olives, vegetables with almonds and pistachios – as well as excellent grilled meat platters and herb-strewn salads. Wash everything down with mint tea or the house beer – made especially for the restaurant by local microbrewery La Brasserie de la Goutte d'Or.

8.

CHEZ CAMILLE

8 rue Ravignan, 18e
01 42 57 75 62
Open Tues–Sun 6pm–2am
Metro: Abbesses, Pigalle

Trade the crowds traipsing up Sacré-Cœur's steps for this slice of Parisian life, along with a view at dusk from its tiny terrace. Okay, so the vista from this bar is not nearly as splendid as it is from the basilica, but the unlikely crowd of fabulously eccentric, young bobos and, yes, the odd stray tourist, is far more fun. There's excellent cheese and charcuterie and quite drinkable wine by the glass, but join everyone else for a house mojito – one of the city's cheapest and, while not what you'd call artisan, there's no skimping on fresh lime and mint. Sunday nights here are laid-back, but it's also when the locals come out to really play.

PARIS TIP

Montmartre's Marché Saint-Pierre is not, in fact, a market but a whole mini-neighbourhood of huge competing fabric emporiums. You'll find every imaginable material available, from Liberty cotton to West African wax-print cloth to fabric used in designer collections.

9.

LE TRÈS PARTICULIER

Hôtel Particulier Montmartre,
Pavillon D, 23 avenue Junot, 18e
01 53 41 81 40
hotel-particulier-montmartre.com
Open Mon–Sun 6pm–2am
Metro: Lamarck-Caulaincourt

There's a pleasing dissonance
of feeling like you're
somewhere quintessentially
Paris of the moment and yet
somewhere totally out of
time at the Hôtel Particulier
Montmartre, a hotel set in
an 18th-century Directoire-
style mansion and possessing
the largest – and lushest –
hotel garden in the city.
Arriving for a drink at its
Le Très Particulier bar can
also feel like embarking on
a mythical quest, your goal
guarded by gates, passages
and the mysterious rocher
de la sorcière – the witch's
rock. Once you've arrived
there are murals of Edenic
forests to sip by, or settle in
the lush, tropical-plant-filled
conservatory. Cocktails, like
the l'Egoïste's mix of gin,
lemon thyme, chamomile
and smoked tea, are highly
crafted, and rather dreamlike too.

TO
MAP RIGHT
(VIA RUE DES
PYRÉNÉES)

The 19e and 20e were, for most of the 19th century, cheap wine and dancing destinations, while for much of the next hundred years, they were home to the city's workers and immigrants. More recently, the bobos have claimed Belleville and Ménilmontant, while Chinese and North African communities continue to thrive here too.

That 19th-century, party-hard spirit lives on in these precincts' many bars, live-music venues and independent galleries, while former industrial powerhouse La Villette has been transformed into a green, waterfront entertainment zone. The north-east's surprisingly green spaces – hilly Parc de Belleville and the rambling Parc des Buttes Chaumont – have splendid views aplenty.

24   JUN 8076

EAT
1 CREAM
EAT AND DRINK
2 CAFÉ CACHÉ
3 ROSA BONHEUR
4 MAMA SHELTER
5 LA BELLEVILLOISE
6 LE 25°EST

17

DRINK
7 BAROURCQ
8 LA FÉLINE
9 LA FLÈCHE D'OR

19E AND 20E:
BELLEVILLE AND
MÉNILMONTANT

1.

CREAM

50 rue de Belleville, 20e
09 83 66 58 43
cream-belleville.tumblr.com
Open Mon–Fri 7.30am–6.30pm,
Sat–Sun 8.30am–7.30pm
Metro: Belleville, Pyrénées

Joe and Max were both baristas at Ten Belles (*see* p. 137) before heading up to Belleville to open their own place, so naturally they're brewing old boss Thomas Lehoux' Belleville Brûlerie beans. You can get a pourover coffee here, but the painted mirror menu not only looks like it's Edith Piaf's vintage, it's delightfully old-school France, listing café crème and café noisette, rather than the increasingly common Anglo-Italian cafe latte or macchiato. Beautiful Bellevillians work and play on the locally made industrial-style furniture and woof down piadina wraps and homemade pain d'épice (gingerbread). But what of the anglophone name? It's for the Wu-Tang Clan or Prince song – your choice.

2.

CAFÉ CACHÉ

104 rue d'Aubervilliers, 19e
cafecache.fr
Open Tues–Wed 9am–8pm,
Thurs–Sat 9am–10.30pm,
Sun 11am–8pm
Metro: Riquet

The vast 104 (Centquatre) art centre, set in what was once the City of Paris' undertakers' building, hosts performances and exhibitions, but is also one of the largest artists' residencies in Europe. Café Caché feeds and waters 104's audience, doubles as the resident artists' canteen and is also a local's favourite, making for a vibrant outpost up in this yet-to-gentrify neck of the La Villette neighbourhood. Belgian designer Sebastien Wierinck was a 104 resident when he came up with the café's extreme craft interior, a beautifully realised fit-out that's somehow both warmly nostalgic and futuristic. Snack or feast on smart little Spanish dishes or French comfort food, washed down with good wines, smoothies or fresh juices.

3.

ROSA BONHEUR

2 allée de la Cascade, Parc des Buttes Chaumont (gate 7, opposite 74 rue Botzaris), 19e
01 42 00 00 45
rosabonheur.fr
Open Wed–Fri 12pm–12am,
Sat–Sun 10am–12am
Metro: Buttes Chaumont, Botzaris

Named for the 19th-century landscape painter, whose name serendipitously translates as 'happiness', this is indeed a happy place and one that comes with a landscape almost as bucolic as Rosa's work. Set in an original 1867 guinguette (dance hall/tavern) on the grassy slopes of Parc des Buttes Chaumont, Rosa Bonheur serves up organic picnic food during the day and morphs into a reinvented version of its raucous 19th-century self at night with DJs and dancing. There's always a come-as-you-are atmosphere, fuelled by the owners' southern (as in south of France) sense of hospitality and joie de vivre. Sunday afternoon and evening attract a big, gay crowd – expect long queues or get happy early.

4.

MAMA SHELTER

109 rue de Bagnolet, 20e
01 43 48 45 45
mamashelter.com
Open Mon–Sat 7–11am,
12–3pm & 7pm–1.30am,
Sun 7–11am, 12.30–4.30pm &
7pm–1.30am
Metro: Alexandre Dumas,
Gambetta

Back in 2009, it was a bold, perhaps visionary move to open a Philippe Starck–designed hotel on a nowhere stretch of rue Bagnolet, overlooking la Petit Ceinture, a richly tagged and overgrown former railway line. But Mama Shelter has packed them in from day one, and its low-slung lair of a bar and restaurant still packs them in most nights. The food is tasty (if rarely notable), the cocktails fresh and flowing, and there's an expansive wine-by-the-glass list to choose from. Well-dressed Parisians usually outnumber international guests too, unless it's fashion week or art fair time. But because someone's always staying over upstairs, even Monday nights can have a party vibe.

LA BELLEVILLOISE

19–21 rue Boyer, 20e
01 46 36 07 07
labellevilloise.com
Open Wed–Thurs 6–11pm,
Fri 6pm–2am, Sat 11am–2am,
Sun 11.30am–11pm
Metro: Gambetta

Built in 1877 as the city's first workers' cooperative, a place of organising, educating and, presumably, the odd celebration or two, the Bellevilloise today hosts bands (jazz, Afropop, folk, cabaret, indie), DJs, performances and exhibitions, as well as general good times. You can eat under hundred-year-old olive trees in the rustic Halle aux Oliviers space downstairs, while upstairs there's a terrace with views stretching south over the rooftops of Ménilmontant to all of Paris below – perfect for sunset drinks. The crowd is young, but Sunday brunch (and occasional '80s DJ nights) brings out the older-gen bobos in force.

LA HALLE AUX OLIVIERS
LE CLUB

PARIS TIP
Encircled by high walls and with broad tree-lined avenues, Paris' largest cemetery, Cimetière du Père-Lachaise, feels like a city within a city. Oscar Wilde's touching tomb and Jim Morrison's simple graffiti-daubed grave draw crowds, but you can usually pay your respects to Proust or Piaf in peace.

LE 25°EST

10 Place de la Bataille de
Stalingrad, 19e
01 42 09 66 74
25est.com
Open Mon–Sun 11am–2am
Metro: Jaurès, Stalingrad

Up where Canal Saint-Martin becomes Bassin de la Villette, the old warehouses and workshops of this artificial lake are now home to pieds dans l'eau (waterfront) bars and venues. The Place de Stalingrad's lot have a festive, fun vibe, especially when the sun is out. Le 25°Est has a particularly laid-back charm and a perfect position, with views over the water and across to the 18th-century neoclassical Rotonde (formerly a city gate building, now a bar and nightclub). There's a spectacular rooftop terrace where jugs of beer go down a treat, especially during long summertime sunsets. Downstairs, the pubby menu is well pitched at the young Canal Saint-Martin escapees: homemade, hearty and very, very cheap.

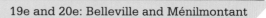

7.

BAROURCQ

68 Quai de la Loire, 19e
01 42 40 12 26
barourcq.free.fr
Open Wed–Thurs 3pm–12am,
Fri–Sat 3pm–2am, Sun 3–10pm
Metro: Laumière, Riquet

You can join a game of canal-side petanque at this super-chilled bar, where regulars grab a plastic cup of pastis and head out for a throw. Impromptu concerts with live music or DJs are also on the cards. If the weather's more Parisian than Provençal, and everyone's moved inside, not to worry. This brightly daubed corner bar is entertaining whatever the weather, with cheap wine, even cheaper snacks, lots of spots to get cosy and even board games. It's also a perfect spot to just quietly admire Bassin de la Villette's rugged industrial beauty, if that's your thing.

8.

LA FÉLINE

6 rue Victor Letalle, 20e
lafelinebar.com
Open Tues–Sat 6pm–2am
Metro: Ménilmontant

Just up from where rue Oberkampf transitions into rue Ménilmontant, this little backstreet bar can show you how Paris does rock'n'roll – that is, with a rockabilly soundtrack, dangerous-looking barmen and much concerted swigging of beer and industrial-strength vodka. Free concerts happen from Thursday to Saturday along with DJ sets, and there are also occasional cult-film screenings. It's the kind of place that announces last-minute secret gigs on its Facebook page – if you and your favourite rock or indie act happen to be in Paris at the same time, it's worth keeping an eye out.

BarOurcq

La Féline

9.

LA FLÈCHE D'OR

102bis rue de Bagnolet, 20e
01 44 64 01 02
flechedor.fr
Open Tues–Fri 8pm–2am,
Sat–Sun 8pm–6am
Metro: Alexandre Dumas,
Gambetta

Paris' music scene is one of its unsung attractions, with any number of local and international acts playing the city on any given night of the week. This is but one of many live-music venues in the mix, but it's a good pick if you're an indie or electro fan. More than that though, it's fabulously atmospheric, set in the old Charonne railway station, and named for the train that once ran to London from here. You can book tickets online, or, depending on the night, just turn up. If it's full house or it's doing one of its occasional shutdowns, the Mama Shelter bar (*see* p. 216) is just across the way.

Creative duo Mario (art director) and Nastassja (fashion PR) are behind the 'anti-left-bank' streetwear label Paris Nord, and have been based in the 18e and 19e for over a decade. Their T-shirts, sloppy joes and hoodies celebrate a new vision of the city's north and take inspiration from 'just around the corner'.

Where do you go for coffee?

Café Caché in the 104 art centre (see p. 214). The 104 is a fantastic place where you can find dancers, kids playing football, art exhibitions, pizza trucks, flea markets, a library and two nice café-restaurants.

What is the best place for a night out?

For a late aperitif, we like to head to Aux Folies in the 20e (see map p. 211) or the rooftop terrace at Le 25°Est (see p. 219). Then we might have Chinese dumplings at Guo Xin in the 19e (see map p. 211) and last beer(s) at La Féline (see p. 220).

What's your favourite Paris (Nord) moment?

La Fête de Ganesh! It's held on a Sunday at the end of August or the beginning of September near the Marx Dormoy metro station in La Chapelle in the 18e. It's a huge commemoration of the Hindu god with massive elephant statues carried through the streets. It is so full of contrasts, joy and coconuts!

Where do you go to escape?

We rent a mini-boat on the Canal de l'Ourcq and 'sail' all the way to Pantin [a north-eastern suburb of Paris].

ARRIVING BY AIR

Charles de Gaulle (CDG)

Paris' major international airport – often referred to by locals as Roissy – is around 30km northeast of the city centre. There are three terminals: 1, 2 and 3. A free light rail, CDGVAL, connects all three terminals. Terminal 2's several subterminals, A to G, are all connected internally, apart from remote 2G. A free shuttle runs from 2F to 2G.

Trains run to Gare du Nord and Châtelet–Les Halles, where you can connect to the metro. The RER B station is located between terminals 2C/2D and 2F/2E.

Air France runs a half-hourly bus service from Étoile and Port Maillot metro stops (€17) and Gare Montparnasse and Gare de Lyon stations (€17.50); both take between one and one and a half hours. It also runs a shuttle between CDG and Orly (€21). Timetables and ticket sales can be found at lescarsairfrance.com. RoissyBus services (€11) leave every 15 to 20 minutes from Opéra train station.

Orly

Paris' second airport is 18km south of Paris. Flights to and from here are mostly domestic, intra-European or to North Africa. There are two terminals: Sud (south) and Ouest (west).

RER B and RER C trains connect to Orly via a shuttle train, Orlyval, and a bus service respectively; RER B/Orlyval costs €12.50, and RER C/bus costs €6.80.

Air France buses also run from Étoile and Champs-Élysées (€12.50), while OrlyBus services (€7.70) leave every 8 to 15 minutes from Denfert-Rochereau metro station. Information can be found at aeroportsdeparis.fr.

Airport taxis

Taxis to and from CDG take around 30 to 60 minutes, depending on the time of day, and cost between €50 to €80, while those to Orly take 20 to 40 minutes and cost around €40. Luggage attracts a €1 surcharge per piece. At the airport do not accept lifts from drivers who approach you – registered, metered taxis will not do this.

WeCab (wecab.com), a taxi-sharing service run by taxi company G7, offers shared taxis both to and from the airport. Prices are fixed. Depending on your arrival or departure address in Paris, these usually cost around €35 for CDG or €25 for Orly. Rides can be booked online in English and there are English-speaking operators. You must have a working mobile phone to confirm your arrival and to receive your pick-up location at the airport, or for the driver to confirm their impending arrival if travelling to the airport.

ARRIVING BY TRAIN

Eurostar services from London and Thalys services from Brussels, Antwerp, Amsterdam and Cologne arrive and depart from Gare du Nord. France's national train service SNCF, which has both domestic and international routes and includes the fast TGV network, arrives into various stations: Gare du Nord, Gare Montparnasse, Gare de l'Est, Gare de Lyon, Bercy, Austerlitz and Gare Saint-Lazare.

Public transport – metro, buses, the RER, trams and the Montmartre funicular – in Paris and its suburbs is run by government company RATP (ratp.fr). The website has dedicated information for tourists in several languages.

RATP's Paris Visite travel card is valid for one, two, three or five consecutive days in zones 1 to 3 or 1 to 5 (includes CDG or Orly). Depending on which zones you choose, it covers all metro travel, RER lines, Transilien SNCF buses, RATP and Optile buses throughout the Ile-de-France, Orlyval and the Montmartre funicular. Tickets can be bought online at metro and RER stations.

Single trip T+ tickets can also be used across the system and can be purchased singly or in packs of ten from metro stations or directly from drivers on buses.

Walking

Walking is a wonderful way to discover Paris. Paris' traffic snarls are often so bad, it can be quicker to walk than take a taxi.

Metro

Metro trains run frequently between 5.30am and 1am, or 2am on Friday and Saturday. Intersecting lines are colour-coded and numbered. It's a good idea to remember the name of the last station in the direction you are going, as this is sometimes the only signage displayed in metro station corridors. RATP's Visiting Paris by Metro app is available for free from the website.

Bus

The Paris Transilien bus network can be daunting, but it provides many shortcuts across the city. Route stops are marked at each bus stop and on buses, which makes things a little easier. At night, when the metro is closed, the Noctilien service takes over. Night buses run every ten to 30 minutes. See vianavigo.com for details.

Vélib

The city's popular bike-share system is one of the world's most extensive. The chunky grey bikes, can be collected and returned to any of the 1000-plus docking stations 24 hours a day. Subscriptions cost €1.70/€8/€29 per day/week/year, which gives you unlimited single 30-minute rental periods. After that you'll be charged €1 to €4 for each subsequent 30-minute period – this rising scale keeps bikes in circulation. Subscribe online (velib.paris) or at any docking station.

Batobus

This tourist boat along the Seine has stops close to many of Paris' major tourist attractions. It's a hop-on, hop-off service and daily passes cost €16.

Taxi

Paris' taxis are cheap by European standards but can be hard to find, especially at peak hour or on weekend evenings. Rooftop lights are green when a taxi is free, red when it's taken, although drivers won't stop if you are within 50 metres of a taxi stand. There is a minimum charge of €7. G7 (taxisG7.fr) is the largest company and has a dedicated English line if you need to book. Uber is popular here and there is a similar local service called Le Cab (lecab.fr).

WI-FI

Cafés and bars often offer wi-fi (pronounced 'wee-fee') and free wi-fi is available in around 300 public places, including parks, major squares and libraries. There's a map and list at paris.fr.

POST

We've all been there: a quick spot of shopping and suddenly you've got a suitcase that's bursting its zips or, worse, baggage allowance blues at the airport. La Poste – the national post office – sells Colissimo boxes that can be posted around the world. These are trackable and can be insured. Check all rates at colissimo.fr.

PUBLIC HOLIDAYS

There are eleven official public holidays in France and four of these fall in May. Parisians often string these together to make longer breaks and this can mean that May weekends in the city are quieter than usual. Transport out of town can also be heavily booked during this period.

TOURIST INFORMATION

Paris Rendezvous (rendezvous.paris.fr; 29 rue de Rivoli, 4e; open Monday to Saturday 10am to 7pm; metro: Hôtel de Ville, Châtelet) is Paris' main tourist information centre.

LOCAL LINGO

apéro: an aperitif, or having a pre-dinner drink.

biologique or bio: organic.

bobo: a contraction of 'bourgeois-bohème'; well-educated, creative young to middle-aged Parisians; often used pejoratively.

branché: literally, 'plugged in' – trendy, cool.

brocante: flea market, bric-a-brac market; often used to describe something as vintage

faire le pont: literally 'to make a bridge'; refers to the habit of taking days off in between public holidays to make extra-long weekends.

hyper: pronounced 'e-pair'; sometimes used instead of 'très' to add emphasis.

les banlieues: literally 'suburbs', though in Paris it usually refers to the city's poorer outer neighbourhoods.

natural wines: wines made using traditional winemaking techniques with minimal or no chemical and technical intervention.

neo-bistro/néo-bistrot: contemporary, informal restaurants offering innovative reworkings of traditional dishes.

Périphérique: Paris' defining ring road.

soixante-huitard: a '68er'; someone who was part of the student and workers' protest movement in 1968, a progressive baby boomer

zinc bar: 'le zinc' is a term used by Émile Zola in his 1873 novel *The Belly of Paris*; refers to both the stainless-steel-topped counter in a bar and the bar itself. The term evokes the idea of a friendly, local place in the same way 'pub' does in English.

While Parisians have a reputation for gruffness, old-fashioned civilities are still the norm here: being polite can really work in your favour. Always extend a 'bonjour madame/monsieur' and 'au revoir' or 'merci' to everyone, from shop assistants to taxi drivers to someone you ask for directions. Do try and use whatever French you have, even if it is just a few words.

Eating out

France, like most of Europe, has set meal times that are followed by restaurants, although this has begun to change in Paris with a number of 'service continu' places that either serve full meals all day or at least a menu of sizeable snacks between lunch and dinner services. Otherwise dinner will rarely be available before 7pm, and most Parisians don't dine before 8pm, often much later. If you're starving, don't hesitate to eat earlier – this is often when you can nab a table at an otherwise hard-to-book place – or follow the local custom of taking an apéro before dinner, either at a bar or a friend's place.

Many restaurants offer fixed-price lunches and dinners, either a two- or three- (or more) course menu or 'une formule', usually a simpler and cheaper meal. These often great value.

Paris' waiters have a reputation for surliness but, while you'll come across at least one example of the stereotype, there's also a new breed of staff that are unfailingly charming and helpful. Be respectful and polite whatever the case.

It's considered bad form to request changes to dishes based on likes and dislikes. You are there to eat what the chef – a highly regarded professional – has prepared. That said, restaurant staff are increasingly aware of food intolerances and will often be able to suggest a dish that is suitable or perhaps minor modifications, like serving a sauce on the side, if you ask nicely.

You'll need to request the bill (l'addition, s'il vous plaît) when you are finished. Service charges are included, so tipping is not obligatory, however, a tip of anything from 5% to 10%, or rounding up in more casual places, will be appreciated (and is wise if you intend to return).

Eating 'sans gluten' can be tricky with wheat flour hiding in many sauces. There are, however, a number of excellent gluten-free bakers and cafes across the city, including Helmut Newcake (36 rue Bichat, 10e), Chambelland Boulangerie (14 rue Terneux, 11e), Noglu Restaurant & Épicerie (16 passage des Panoramas, 2e) and Thank You, My Deer (112 rue Saint-Maur, 11e).

Coffee

Paris' many 'third-wave' or Anglo-style cafes usually serve coffee with a similar nomenclature to their counterparts in the US, Australia and the UK. Most will, however, call an espresso 'un café' and a long black an Americano.

Traditional French coffee terminology still holds sway in neighbourhood bars and more traditional cafés and includes:

- le café au lait: coffee with milk

- un café crème, un crème: espresso with hot milk; like a cafe latte, but usually weaker

- un café noisette, une noisette: espresso with a dash of milk or a spoonful of foam, similar to a macchiato

- un café américain, café noir, café allongé: long black, weak black coffee

- déca, Hag: the suffix for decaf coffee (Hag is a brand)

- café Cognac: booze-laden short black

ABOUT THE AUTHOR

Donna Wheeler

Paris was the very first place Donna visited beyond her native Australia. Not long out of art school, it was a life-changing trip, full of swoons, both literal and figurative, where she drank in the Ingres and Delacroixs, the Bonnards and the Atgets; wolfed down clafouti and couscous and Chablis; bought Robert Clergerie shoes she could not afford; and spent endless hours name checking everything she'd ever read or seen in movies.

After a long absence, she returned to Paris in 2006 and has been a constant visitor and sometime semi-resident ever since. The city has been her base while working on guidebooks and a host of other travel assignments in France, North Africa, Italy, Belgium, Austria and Scandinavia. While she has never lost the giddy sense of excitement that marked her first stay, that breathless fascination has grown into an enduring love as she's come to see the city in its many moods and seasons, gradually uncovering its many nuances and complexities.

ACKNOWLEDGEMENTS

Thanks to Hardie Grant's Melissa Kayser for 'getting' my vision of Paris, to Alison Proietto for her sharp thinking and steady stewardship along with her patience and pep talks, to Michelle Bennett for her careful and tireless editing. Thanks also to Michelle Mackintosh, Emily Maffei and Megan Ellis for all their work in helping to create this beautiful book.

On the ground in Paris, many thanks go to Patrick Nectoux for such big-hearted hospitality; Laurence Billiet and Rachael Antony for the convivial dinners and coffee dates; Gwen Jamois for the muscadet, music and kindness; Jean-Bernard Carillet for your Left Bank intel; Juliette Clare for the lovely afternoons; Tariq Krim for your friendship and generosity; Florence Lopez for the warmest of welcomes; Emily Mazo-Rizzi for keeping me flexible; and Alex Landragin for the inspiring conversations and last-minute vocab help. Thanks to honorary Parisian Daniel Nettheim, too, for hacking the travel writer pace and, as always, your lovely company. Retrospective thanks go to Dr Chris Brasher, whose own richly layered and occasionally dissolute version of Paris has so informed my own.

Back in Australia, much love goes to my daughters, Rumer and Biba, and my husband, Joe Guario, who weather my protracted absences with good grace and great faith. I'm also ever grateful to those who've kept my spirits buoyed from afar and/or have given me a quiet place to write and think: Sam Ashby, Cristian Bonetto, Kate Dale, Darryn Devlin, Brigid Healy, Andrew King, Karen Radzyner, Debbie Wheeler and Nicholas Wrathall.

This book is for my lifelong friend, Rebecca Brandon: yes, my darling, we will always have Paris.

The publisher would like to acknowledge the following individuals and organisations:

Editorial manager
Marg Bowman

Project manager
Alison Proietto

Editor
Michelle Bennett

Cartography
Emily Maffei

Design
Michelle Mackintosh

Layout
Megan Ellis

Index
Max McMaster

Pre-press
Megan Ellis, Splitting Image

Photography credits

All photos © Donna Wheeler, except for the following (letters indicate where multiple images appear on a page, from top to bottom, left to right):

Pages 8 (a), 9 (a) & (b) courtesy of Épice; 16 courtesy Yasmin Eslami; 24 Danielle Rubi; 26–27 Jérôme Galland; 30 (a), 31 (b) & (c) Paul Bowyer; 48 (a) & 49 (a) courtesy of 404; 52 courtesy of Antoine Ricardou; 59 Laura Lot; 60–61 Pierre Monetta; 62 courtesy of Tariq Krim; 74 Ola Rindal; 80 (a) & 81 (a) courtesy of Assouline; 80 (b) & 81 (b) Phillipe Garcia; 87 (a) & (c) UgoRichard; 87 (b) Addie Chinn; 88 courtesy of Florence Lopez; 93 courtesy of India Mahdavi; 94 (b) S. Delpech; 95 (a) & (c) DosSantos Lemone; 96–97 Gourmet TV Productions; 98 Rina Nurra; 100–101 courtesy of Coutume; 107 Nicolas Matheus; 108–109 courtesy of Four Seasons; 116 Gaspard Hermach; 126 (b), 127 (a), (e) & (f) Diane Yoon; 128 courtesy of Clotilde DuSoulier; 132 (a), 133 (a) & (b) Laurence Peyrelade; 141 courtesy of Vivant; 146 Nicol Despis; 150 Olivier Laly; 152 Pierre Monetta; 153 PilmliCom; 162 Johanna Heather Anselmo; 168, 170 (b), 171 (a), (b), (c) & (f) Daniel Nettheim; 170 (a), 171 (d), (e) Renaud Cambuzat; 174 courtesy of Daran Fulham; 182 (a) & 183 courtesy Nüba; 182 (b) Laura Lot; 184 courtesy of Vanessa Scoffier; 189 (a) Cheung-Leng Tran; 189 (d), (e) & (f) Sébastien Racineux; 192–193 Thomas Duval; 194 courtesy of Cheung-Leng Tran; 200 (b) & 201 courtesy of A.P.C. Surplus; 202 Laura Lot; 208–209 Jefferson Lellouche; 216–217 Francis Amiand; 220(a) & 221 (a) Matthieu Doze; 220 (b) & 221 (b) Laura lot; 222–223 courtesy of La Fléche d'Or; 224 courtesy of Paris Nord.

Explore Australia Publishing Pty Ltd
Ground Floor, Building 1, 658 Church Street,
Richmond, VIC 3121, Australia

Explore Australia Publishing Pty Ltd is a division of Hardie Grant Publishing Pty Ltd

Published by Explore Australia Publishing Pty Ltd, 2016

A Cataloguing-in-Publication entry is available from the catalogue of the National Library of Australia at www.nla.gov.au

ISBN-13 9781741174984

10 9 8 7 6 5 4 3 2 1

Printed and bound in China by 1010 Printing International Ltd

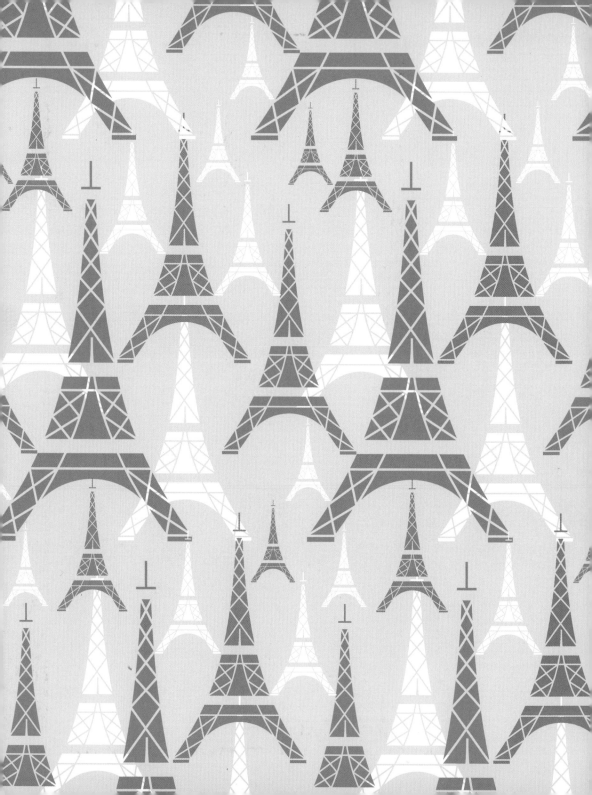